T0285986

FLORIDA SPECTACULAR

UNIVERSITY PRESS OF FLORIDA

Florida A&M University, Tallahassee
Florida Atlantic University, Boca Raton
Florida Gulf Coast University, Ft. Myers
Florida International University, Miami
Florida State University, Tallahassee
New College of Florida, Sarasota
University of Central Florida, Orlando
University of Florida, Gainesville
University of North Florida, Jacksonville
University of South Florida, Tampa
University of West Florida, Pensacola

FLORIDA SPECTACULAR

Extraordinary Places and Exceptional Lives

CATHY SALUSTRI

UNIVERSITY PRESS OF FLORIDA

Gainesville · Tallahassee · Tampa · Boca Raton
Pensacola · Orlando · Miami · Jacksonville · Ft. Myers · Sarasota

29 28 27 26 25 24   6 5 4 3 2 1

Library of Congress Cataloging-in-Publication Data
Names: Salustri, Cathy, author.
Title: Florida spectacular : extraordinary places and exceptional lives / Cathy Salustri.
Description: Gainesville : University Press of Florida, [2024] | Includes bibliographical references
and index. | Summary: "Explaining why the state is more than the "Florida Man" stories and other
stereotypes, this book celebrates what makes Florida worth a deeper understanding in a lively trip
through the state's natural beauty and fascinating history"— Provided by publisher.
Identifiers: LCCN 2024007585 | ISBN 9780813080697 (paperback) | ISBN 9780813073408
(ebook)
Subjects: LCSH: Natural history—Florida. | Curiosities and wonders—Florida. | Florida—
Description and travel. | Florida—History. | BISAC: HISTORY / United States / State & Local /
South (AL, AR, FL, GA, KY, LA, MS, NC, SC, TN, VA, WV)
Classification: LCC F311 .S253 2024 | DDC 917.5904—dc23/eng/20240313
LC record available at https://lccn.loc.gov/2024007585

The University Press of Florida is the scholarly publishing agency for the State University System
of Florida, comprising Florida A&M University, Florida Atlantic University, Florida Gulf Coast
University, Florida International University, Florida State University, New College of Florida, University of Central Florida, University of Florida, University of North Florida, University of South
Florida, and University of West Florida.

University Press of Florida
2046 NE Waldo Road
Suite 2100
Gainesville, FL 32609
http://upress.ufl.edu

CONTENTS

Introduction

Florida-splaining, Conch Shells, and Bubbly

March 2019

I'm standing in David Sloan's kitchen, and we're all drinking out of a conch shell. David and his partner, Heather May, live on Stock Island, the forgotten key north and east of Key West that most tourists will not notice, much less visit. As an après-brunch treat, he's lured us back to his scrap of paradise with the promise of key lime pie on a stick and conch shell champagne.

My friend Brad Bertelli, a fellow author and former curator at the Keys History & Discovery Center in Islamorada, thought I'd like David, so Brad arranged a meeting. David created a Key West ghost tour, organizes the annual Cow Key Channel Zero K Bridge Run, and writes about the wonders of Key West and the Florida Keys. He's also an intrepid Key West historian, publishing tales of Bum Farto and other notables in the local paper.

"This," he says, "will become a Key West tradition."

As David pops the cork, I find myself about to refuse. Champagne and all its relatives give me a headache. Then David pulls out a massive queen conch shell, the kind you hold up to your ear to hear the ocean, and pours low-priced sparkling white wine into it. He passes the shell first to Heather May, who takes a sip and passes it to my husband, Barry. When Barry passes it to me, I underestimate how quickly liquid runs out of a conch shell and the bubbles go up my nose as the cold hits the back of my throat, and I start to laugh and try not to spit wine back into the shell. I pass the shell to Michelle, who partakes far more delicately than I, then passes it to her husband, Brad, who's looking pleased with his idea that we should all meet. As I head to the sink to wash the excess bubbly off my face and hands, I'm smiling. Brad was right—I'm thrilled to know David, and, thanks to them both, I'm having a quintessential Florida day.

I'm in town to sign books at Judy Blume's bookstore, Books and Books Key West, but no one's offering to put me up in the Heron House or the Waldorf Astoria, or even the Holiday Inn. Key West hotels cost money our family's writer-and-boat-captain budget won't allow, so we've booked ourselves on Stock Island at the Perry, a hotel made to look simultaneously upscale and vintage. Stock Island belongs to the working class, the laborers who make a living off the tourists one key over. I'm unclear on how Stock Island got its name—conventional wisdom suggests it has something to do with livestock pens—but I do know that for years, you didn't go there unless you wanted a boat motor fixed, worked in a boatyard, or had plans that may have strayed from traditional interpretations of "legal." The small key had a reputation for its unvarnished inhabitants who were not at all interested in giving tourists a wonderful experience. So severe was the behavior on Stock Island that it was a natural place to dump a body—as happened in Tom Corcoran's *Bone Island Mambo*.

But just as Key West has changed, so has Stock Island, and today, Stock Island's a treasure. My morning run takes me past the boatyard to the water's edge. Our hotel abuts a liveaboard marina, so locals outnumber tourists at the hotel restaurant and bar. That bar, by the way, allows dogs, and not only on the patio; I see one on a barstool and do a double take and his owner confirms: he's the dog on our room's Do Not Disturb sign.

Because it's Stock Island and not Key West proper, I don't have a wide array of dining choices; it's either the Perry's restaurant, El Siboney, or Hogfish Grill. While not technically in Key West, every time I've eaten at Hogfish, it's the best time I've had in Key West. Nothing about the restaurant or the company feels like spectacle. Sandwiched into the marina across from pallets of construction supplies, trailers, and trash along Front Street, Hogfish serves food that costs slightly less and tastes *more* than slightly better, and the atmosphere's organic rather than contrived in a boardroom by a restaurant conglomerate.

Earlier in the day, David led us behind Hogfish Grill to introduce us to the artists living and working on the mismatched flotilla of houseboats hidden there. The houseboats aren't fancy; these aren't formal galleries, but studios and homes that happen to float in a hidden colony. This is about as far away as you can get from Key West, the place where, once upon a not-too-distant time, you could watch a stripper put matches in her nipples and light them (the matches, not the nipples)—steps away from the largest Cuban cultural center in the United States. My husband says it best: Key West went to hell when it built a Dunkin' Donuts. People bemoan the loss of Key West to the cruise ships, but on this trip I've learned that the real Conchs (that's what Key West natives and veterans call themselves) find the real Key West in the places most tourists wouldn't dare look. These houseboats are one such instance.

David's peeling back the curtain on the Key West I thought long gone.

Before America had tiny homes, Florida had mobile homes, and David and Heather May have maximized the space so that there's a writing studio in the back (David's book titles range from *Quit Your Job and Move to Key West: The Complete Guide* to *Roosters Are Assholes*, which summarizes the way people feel moving to and away from the Keys, in my experience); a formal living room with a couch boasting broad, colonial stripes; and a family room that looks like something out of an especially artistic Spencer's gift store, circa 1987, with guitars and album art and odd bits of Florida funk curated on the walls.

Elsewhere, they have a chest freezer brimming with frozen key lime pie pops, and a kitchen easily as big as both living rooms. In the bathroom, they have a Squatty Potty. On the lawn—if you can call it that, which, spoiler alert, you can't in the Keys—plastic dinosaurs and a black metal horse guard the homestead. One of the many chickens that gravitate toward the Sloan household, Cluck Norris, waits on a chicken swing. In the backyard we find a Skunk Ape statue, foam buoys in red and yellow and green and white and green and orange, and a full-size electric sign boasting BAIT in bold, red, vertical letters. Chickens avoid the panting Orca, their boxy black dog, who'd rather not be doing much of anything, thank you. Those same chickens play the xylophone for treats. It's a colorful explosion of a home that makes you feel Florida in your bones.

Get a group of Florida writers together and one thing's certain: we are going to tell Florida stories. At the restaurant, among the houseboats, and in David's kitchen, we're trading stories again. For Florida-philes, nothing compares to finding Florida fans and talking about our beloved state. We relish telling someone new all our favorite anecdotes, like the one where we got lost in the swamp and almost died from snakebite (see chapter 10) or the one where Florida alone saves the last big cat east of the Mississippi River from extinction (chapter 8). When we find someone who loves the Sunshine State as much as we do, one who gets that look in their eye when you tell your Florida stories, well, the joy is palpable. That's when we come alive.

And so that afternoon in the kitchen, our sextet talks about the Overseas Railroad and the two Henrys, and real peeps (Cluck Norris has an entourage), and the Everglades. We talk a lot about Key West; David's the authority on Robert the Doll, Brad's the authority on Indian Key, and I love to talk about the WPA's influence on Cayo Hueso. We talk about Fred, the renegade Australian pine who's steadfastly refused to die on the crumbling Seven Mile Bridge.

"Everybody knows about that tree," Barry interjects. "It's not just a Salustri thing." This is how my husband refers to the Florida things about which I am most passionate: Salustri things.

About Fred? He's not wrong: Brad and David and the Florida Keys tourism bureau all know about Fred. Fred's a rock star, a celebrity in a place that Ernest Hemingway, Hunter S. Thompson, and Tennessee Williams all called home. We talk about Fred and Hurricane Irma and Pigeon Key.

This is how it goes: we Florida-splain. Just as much as we love to share Florida stories, we love to hear them. Give me a cold beer and a back porch and ask me about the Army Corps of Engineers and the Kissimmee River, and you've made my afternoon. Take a cold beer for yourself and tell me about Indian Key's stint as the capital of Dade County, and you've made my afternoon all over again.

We talk about the Labor Day Hurricane of 1935, and then that leads to—of course—the Hurricane of 1928, and then back to Hurricane Irma. We talk about crocodiles, alligators, and indigo snakes. We trade stories about Archbold Biological Station and the Cow Key Run, about the Citrus Tower and pirates and rum distilleries and World War I veterans.

We do not speak of "Margaritaville" or news headlines. We do talk about Key West Pinks, Royal Reds, and sour orange pie. Florida's a rainbow of colors and stories and histories, and once you know the stories, those colors swirl together and paint a breathtaking image. We pass the shell a second time.

Over the next thirteen chapters, come with me to find such moments as I tell you some Florida stories, tales that showcase Florida's spectacular side. Throughout this book, I want to bring you into that kitchen with me. Let's take a trip through Florida together, just you and me, and discover what makes Florida, as this book claims, spectacular. Down with the horrid tales of weird Florida; let's celebrate our amazing, wonderful state.

After you read this book, the next time you're at a dinner party and the talk turns to weird Florida, do a little Florida-splaining of your own. Over dessert, let your dining companions know that the rest of the country looks to Florida for guidance on how to create a wildlife corridor, or that Walt Disney World is actually doing more to restore the Everglades than the federal government, or that—well, you get the idea. The point is, you'll be preaching the gospel of Florida, spreading the best parts of this state far and wide. You'll swallow that last bite of dinner, put down your fork, and excuse yourself.

And then, I hope, you'll go find a conch shell and drink your wine out of it.

I

Florida Springs

An Exploration of Our Watery Treasures

My parents brought me to the state as a seven-year-old refugee from New York. My life now gives no indication of this, but even as I soaked in Florida and all its glorious bounty as a child, part of me always assumed I would move back to New York. I graduated high school and grudgingly spent two years at a local junior college. I didn't want to go to junior college; I wanted to go to NYU. My mother reminded me, gently at first and then with more determination as I became increasingly recalcitrant, that my scholarship would pay for my first three years of a state college and there was no reason I needed to throw the family into debt. My lackluster grades and overall immaturity may have factored into her not wanting to send a seventeen-year-old to Manhattan alone. In retrospect, she was right. After all, what did I know? *I was seventeen.* I thought I was going to marry my high school boyfriend, a former wrestler whose nickname was Rambo, have a business career (and no, I had no grasp of what that meant, just that I was going to "have a business career"), and birth babies. I'd started attending a fundamentalist church, had joined the choir, and was president of the youth group. Now, there's nothing wrong with spirituality, but we're Catholic. That's pretty much the easiest religion there is, and *I'd dropped out.* Fundamentalism was my rebellion. Some teenagers did drugs; I converted to Nazarene. Even now, I can't explain my thought process except to say I really disliked the Catholic Church, but I missed the youth group. See, the Catholic youth group is where I discovered Florida springs.

The youth group went to the Rainbow River, where the adults set us loose on an army of inner tubes—a bunch of pubescent and prepubescent kids blithely unaware of their own mortality, floating down a translucent green river. We may have had the most mundane of teenaged emotions and angst, but we were having them set against the backdrop of ancient limestone, primeval trees, and water gushing forth from the center of the earth.

From there, my destiny was set, even if I didn't know it. To this day, I feel most myself in or on the water. I've had part-time jobs as sailboat crew, speedboat crew, and kayak tour guide. When I was floundering in my job as a section editor at an alt-weekly newspaper, my husband and I were talking one night and he was telling me about his day as a boat captain. I burst into tears because I felt partly dead inside without water time. And although for most of my transplanted life in the state I've lived by saltwater, Florida freshwater epitomizes the state for me. Which is a little quirky; after all, only twenty of our fifty states have any saltwater coastline, and Florida has two. Every state has lakes and rivers, and springs themselves aren't exactly a rarity. But Florida springs—we have more springs than anywhere else on the planet. Plus, ours aren't geothermal. No, our springs are cooling and refreshing, not heated and roiling. The temperature isn't all that's different; everything about these mystical Florida springs differs from their northern cousins.

The first time Barry and I traveled to a Florida spring together, we arrived with vastly different expectations. After spending my teen years tubing down the Rainbow River, in college I'd kayaked across the glass top of Wekiwa Springs. As an adult, I'd scuba dived at Devil's Den. For his part, he had heard me rail about risks to the springs but, not having arrived in Florida until his thirties, had never visited a springhead. He'd spent a good bit of time on saltwater and kayaking blackwater rivers, but no time at all at springheads.

While I can't remember the exact first time I saw a spring, I'll carry with me to the grave the look on Barry's face when he saw Wekiwa Springs. I was working on *Backroads of Paradise*, and we'd made camp at Wekiwa Springs State Park for the night. We were racing a midsummer storm (midsummer in Florida being, of course, September), but we took the time to visit the spring's edge and walk down the steps into the spring. He didn't say anything for a long moment, but then he turned his gaze from the water to me.

"I had no idea," was all he said. While he'd recently enough seen two other springs—Manatee Springs and Three Sisters—they didn't register with him. Manatee Springs is, in fact, a more voluminous spring than

Wekiwa, as are the Crystal Springs group of springs, of which Three Sisters are three.[1] For some reason, though—he later speculated it might have been the spa-like feel of the spring, with a boardwalk and benches on the bank—he reacted viscerally.

This sharp reaction to our springs reminds me of walking through an animal shelter, looking for a dog or a cat: you can walk by ten, twenty, fifty animals, all adorable, all loving and needing love, and for some reason, you'll see this one dog, and you'll stop. He might have only three legs, he might be conventionally ugly, but something in your head whispers, "This one." And that's it; your life is forever changed. I'm not saying after seeing Wekiwa Springs, Barry's life changed in some sweeping way, but it was clear that afternoon he'd seen something he'd never forget, and that Wekiwa Springs had introduced him to part of Florida with which he was not familiar.

That's not so unusual; the springs are so often tucked away between woods and rivers that stumbling across something unexpected can make the person discovering it feel bonded to Florida, as if they and the state share a secret.

As much as I see them, I still marvel when I see a spring, no matter the size. When I first visited Three Sisters, while walking toward the springhead, I stepped over sand and bottom and realized all around my feet were tiny vents and boils, the most minuscule of springs, bubbling up. I stopped, trying to put my toes over the pinholes and marveling at the smallness of the miracle. I would have contented myself with going no farther that afternoon; I could have played with the Lilliputian springs for hours and never have tired of the bitty streams issuing forth.

Springs, in many ways, don't make sense. Think about Florida for a moment—no one accuses our state of having too much elevation. A common misconception is that we're a flat state. That's not accurate; we may not have mountains, or hills, even, but we're far from flat. Our *highest* point may be 345 feet (Britton Hill, in the Panhandle), and yes, that's not only the lowest high point of any state, it's lower than sixteen states' low points. Don't let that fool you into thinking all Florida exists on one level; we do not. Consider a spring: The source of a spring can go down 2,000 feet below the surface. To reach us, spring water must climb a mountain. Think of our Floridan Aquifer as a giant, dark sea, encased in a tunnel of fossilized coral, running 2,000 feet beneath our feet, and we're living atop the peak of those limestone mountains stretching out of our ocean. And, unlike mountains elsewhere in our country, these are magical mountains, because the purest water on the planet runs up them to meet us.

Florida springs enchant, because they defy what we know. They're holes in the surface of the earth that go down deeper than the state ever goes up. And in a state known for our salty surf and sandy beaches, the springs are freshwater pools lined with limestone rock. They depict a whole different world than our beach culture. Our beaches are relaxation and margaritas and sunsets. Our springs? Well, they're all secrets and scotch and whispers. They're magic Florida.

But how did they get there in the first place? Science tells us comets and asteroids brought the individual elements of water to the surface of the earth, but it was once here that they combined into water, and our planet's gravity sucked it down toward the center of the earth, and because limestone lies underneath Florida, gravity pulled more water toward the center of the earth than it would have had we, say, granite lying under our feet. So wherever there was a crack in the surface, water leaked through the limestone, which is the same fossilized coral and marine life that encases that underwater river, the Floridan Aquifer.

Limestone is a spongy, sedimentary rock with some pretty nifty origins. We have limestone because it comes from the skeletons of fish and shrimp and scallops and coral, and Florida used to be much smaller (we used to be much larger, too, but more on that in a bit), so we're talking about roughly 530 million years of sea life dying and decomposing and getting compressed into limestone. On top of that limestone we have a layer of quartz sand that flows down from the Appalachians as they erode (which has been going on for more than 400 million years). This all means when you're playing at the pool at your hotel room, or walking around a park, you're playing and walking on several thousand feet of geologic and oceanic history. Just the right ingredients had to go into the batter to make the state, and without it we wouldn't have our aquifer, without which we couldn't have—in addition to some other things—our springs.

The Floridan Aquifer is a giant underwater river that lies under the northern half of the state and also under parts of Alabama, Georgia, South Carolina, and a tiny sliver of eastern Mississippi. In all, it lies underneath roughly 100,000 miles of the southeastern United States, all of it encased in that limestone, and that limestone is filled with nooks and crannies that form pockets that soak in water— and hold it there.

Let's chat for a second about Florida's drinking water, because I grew up drinking it (well before the advent of bottled water), and though I don't find anything odd with the taste, plenty of newbie Floridians think our water tastes odd. That's because limestone contains calcium and magnesium. While some have trouble adjusting to the taste, think about the supplements doctors often suggest: calcium. Think of Florida's drinking water as the country's first vitamin water, only far less expensive.

If you read much of the scientific writing about the Floridan Aquifer, you'll notice after a bit it sounds a bit like bragging as hydrologists, time and time again, call the Floridan Aquifer "one of the most productive aquifers in the world."[2] How much water does the aquifer hold? About a quadrillion gallons, which is such a huge number it sounds totally made up. Think of it as 20 percent of the Great Lakes,[3] but also like this: in 1988, Floridians, Florida agriculture, and Florida industries pumped more than 3 billion gallons of water *per day* out of the Floridan Aquifer,[4] with little noticeable difference in the water table. That doesn't mean the aquifer can sustain that level of withdrawal indefinitely, but it does help put its size in perspective.

The aquifer does more than act as free storage for drinking water—it also purifies that drinking water. As water falls to earth (usually as rain—at least, in Florida), it soaks into the ground, and gravity pulls it toward the aquifer. It filters through layers of soil, sand, and clay before seeping into the limestone in a process called percolation, and as it percolates, those layers filter the contaminants from the water, producing some of the cleanest drinking water in the country. That's also because the Floridan Aquifer is so deep that the water has to pass through a lot of layers, and as it does, each layer removes more and more contaminants. Percolation is not a fast process, either—hydrologists estimate it takes about a century for rainwater to make it down to the Floridan Aquifer, and some estimates suggest the aquifer has water in it that's been there for twenty-six thousand years.

How does that water get back to the surface? Pressure. Deep aquifers like the Floridan are considered "confined," meaning they're pressurized because the water is encased in limestone, which holds it in place. But limestone doesn't last forever, and acids in water can erode it, and when there's any opening at all on the surface of the earth, if that opening reaches down to the aquifer, the artesian pressure in the aquifer pushes the water to the surface. The difference between an artesian well and a spring is that although they both have underground pressure pushing the water out, an artesian well is a man-made hole, and a spring is where the water finds a hole that already exists.

Springs themselves have several different types: river rises, single springs, group springs, and sinkholes. A river rise refers to an underground river that ultimately rises to the surface. A fantastic example of this is appropriately named River Rise Preserve State Park in North Florida, where the Santa Fe River, a 75-mile-long river, reappears 3 miles away from O'Leno State Park, where it slips underground.

A single spring, much like the river rise, has a fairly straightforward name, because a single spring has one source—although it may poke through the earth at several places. Wakulla Springs, where filmmakers filmed parts of *Tarzan* and *Creature from the Black Lagoon*, is a single spring. A group spring has several underground sources but may flow to a common location, as happens with Kings Bay and Three Sisters, which feed Crystal River, so popular for viewing (and swimming with) manatees.

The final type of spring, known as a sink, has a tarnished reputation. The news loves to report on sinkholes that swallow homes, and yes, while they can do that, they don't usually. A sink occurs when limestone dissolves and the ground simply sinks down far enough that water from the confined aquifer can reach the surface. Usually these sinks include a series of underground sinkholes and caves, which can collapse, also causing a sink. And yes, sinks can also occur when we pump too much water out of the aquifer, but more common is the naturally occurring sink at a low point in the water basin, because that's where most of the rain will collect, so it will dissolve more quickly (or unevenly) here. Devil's Den, which offers some spectacular primeval snorkeling near the University of Florida, is a sink.

Florida's springs come in all sizes—from more than 100 cubic feet per second to one pint of water per minute. You might hear people talk about a "first-magnitude" or "second-magnitude" spring, but what does that mean? A first-magnitude spring is a spring that flows up to your feet at more than 100 cubic feet per second, or 64.6 million gallons per day; by contrast, an eighth-magnitude spring pushes out about one pint of water a minute. All you really need to know is that the lower the number, the more water a spring pushes out from the earth. Florida has thirty-three first-magnitude springs, probably about two hundred second-magnitude springs, and more than seven hundred others (and quite likely more we don't even know about). We have more than any other state—and more than most other countries. Why? It has to do with our geology, weather, and underground water flow. Most of all, it has to do with limestone, because that pockmarked limestone makes it easy for water to "hang out" in all its secret places, the nooks and crannies that act like a sponge. Weather helps, too; Florida gets between 30 and 100 inches of rain per year, and that rain recharges the aquifer.

The Floridan Aquifer also discharges into the Gulf of Mexico and the Atlantic, which creates just the right combination of brackish water crucial for fish nurseries and, consequently, the estuaries where so much of our marine life begins. Although the Floridan Aquifer isn't nearly as deep in coastal regions, it's not unusual to find a freshwater spring quite close to the beach, and you can still find freshwater springs in the Gulf of Mexico and the Atlantic. This is because Florida's west coast extended much farther out during the last ice age—some 100 miles in parts—and so the ground, when exposed, had rainwater that would percolate down and dissolve the limestone. Just because the ground is now covered with saltwater doesn't mean the holes have disappeared. The pressure from the confined aquifer pushes freshwater out of the hole, and the force of that pressure keeps saltwater at bay. You'll only find those springs to the edge of the continental shelf, about 100 miles away, because that's where the limestone ends.

Of course, our springs face challenges, too—and the biggest threat comes from our nice, green lawns. People who move to Florida from up north learn fast that grass doesn't grow as easily here as it did back home. Florida isn't an ideal place for grass for a few reasons. One, it takes a ton of water—literally. But that isn't enough; everything *but* turfgrass loves to grow in Florida, it seems, so to get that lush, green lawn, people need herbicides to kill dollar weed, Spanish bayonet, hatpin, sandspurs, and all sorts of other Florida plants that really would like to grow in your yard. Plus we have chinch bugs and other bugs that like to eat grass, so we put pesticides on our lawns. And, of course, we have to fertilize so the lawn will grow. The end result is a verdant, green lawn—

but there's another effect. All those chemicals don't stay on the ground. When it rains, they percolate into the aquifer along with the rainwater. That means nitrogen, ammonia, benzene, and a host of other toxins with impressive-sounding names are headed right for our drinking water. Now, in Florida, we're lucky, because our aquifer is so deep that usually it can filter many—but not all—of these toxins from the water before it reaches the depths from where we pump our drinking water. There is a concern that we're adding them so fast that the aquifer might not be able to keep up. If it can't, those springs change forever. Our springs face another danger from these chemicals and its runoff: When you fertilize your lawn, you probably don't think much about what happens to that fertilizer after it helps your grass grow. When it rains, the fertilizer washes away, running over the ground along with the rainwater, finding the lowest points. Those lowest points are often springs and sinks. Fertilizer makes everything grow, so when it reaches the springs—or any body of water—it makes whatever greenery lives there grow *more*. That's how we get algae blooms and other types of unpleasantness in the springs. These chemicals can also deprive the water of oxygen, causing fish kills. This changes the makeup of the flora and fauna that comprise the spring.

Protecting the springs falls to every Floridian, and many do what they can, from swearing off bottled water (as have I, and as has Pulitzer Prize–winning author Jack Davis), to ripping out fertilizer-loving turfgrass (as have Barry and I), to lobbying their elected officials (as do countless organizations, such as the Sierra Club). Fighting to keep our springs pure makes sense from an environmental standpoint, but there's something more: Florida's springs create their own wonder.

Peacock Springs, in the north part of the state, near a town called Live Oak, says it all with its name: our springs are an ostentation of colors, prismatic, enchanting, almost magical—and spectacular.

2

Forgotten Colonies

East and West Florida

While Floridians associate springs with kayaking or snorkeling, people across America have heard another tale of our springs, one involving Juan Ponce de León and his ill-fated search for the Fountain of Youth. Of course, it's not true—it was written by the sixteenth-century equivalent of Andy Borowitz, as satire to poke fun at how dumb Ponce de León was. Of course, if something gets repeated enough, it doesn't take long for it to become "fact" in the public mind. And so people today believe that Ponce de León explored Florida in search of the Fountain of Youth.

That's why I'm consistently amazed at people who think Florida is somehow "new." Once upon a time I thought I was going to live on a sailboat. In my quest to find an affordable boat, I dragged my friend Frank across Florida to look at them with me. Now, Frank had no more business judging a sailboat's seaworthiness than I did, but he made for a fun traveling companion. He was a Massachusetts boy by birth and breeding, and everything about Florida showed Frank adventure, from Waffle Houses (I had no idea they were so uniquely southern) to our conquistador history. On a trip to St. Augustine to look at a boat I had no business buying, we strolled the streets of the Spanish Quarter. Frank's gaze locked on a historic marker, at which time he turned to me and, with great dismay and discovery on his face, exclaimed, "I didn't realize Florida had *history*." I contained my own dismay. Yes, Frank, I replied, we have history—and it predates northern attitudes about where US history begins.

For example, you likely remember studying the thirteen "original" colonies in grade school. Delaware, Pennsylvania, Massachusetts—our American history books and classes are filled with grand tales of those "original" colonies. Would it shock you if I told you there were not thirteen, but twenty-two original colonies? Seven of those "extra" nine colonies became part of present-day Canada in the mid-nineteenth century, but what about the other two?

In most of our elementary and high school history classes, Florida seems like an afterthought to American history, but the state we now call Florida has served as a political Ping-Pong ball since the Renaissance, earlier than any other colonial settlement in the United States. From the fourteenth to seventeenth centuries, the European world was dazzled by Renaissance art and Renaissance men, but there's another component that we often overlook in favor of Dante, Leonardo, and Michelangelo: navigation and geography. It was during the Renaissance that European explorers visited every continent except Antarctica. Shifting political boundaries also demanded new trade routes, which is how, during this time period, Europe became the Old World as explorers "discovered" a new one. And Florida was the gateway to that so-called New World.

Think about Florida's European beginnings and what was happening elsewhere in the world. In 1513, Ponce de León gets credit for "discovering" Florida, but earlier maps exist depicting a crude outline of the state. A 1502 map, known as the Cantino Planisphere, comes to us from Alberto Cantino, and it shows Florida. Cantino was an Italian spy working in Portugal, and, according to one version of the story about the map, he used the Duke of Ferrara's money—the duke was his boss—to pay a mapmaker to sneak into a Portuguese map facility to use the maps to create it. According to another version of the story, Cantino simply used his boss's wealth to buy the map. Either way, what we have as a result is a map of Florida that predates Ponce de León by more than a decade.

Right between these two dates—the 1502 Cantino Planisphere and Ponce de León's 1513 discovery of Florida—was when Michelangelo painted the ceiling of the Sistine Chapel. Europeans discovered Florida—or believe they did (the ancestors of the Seminole and Miccosukee came to Florida and what's now the southeastern US thousands of years before)—by the time Pope Julius "persuaded" Michelangelo to take on the chapel job. The year after the Cantino Planisphere gets revealed, Nostradamus was born.

That Age of Discovery was also the start of the Age of a Ridiculous Amount of Angst over Florida. In *The West Florida Controversy, 1798–1813: A Study in American Diplomacy*, Isaac Joslin Cox lays out how, by the end of the Renaissance, three countries—Spain, France, and Great Britain—had all laid claim to Florida, which, at the time, included land from the Atlantic Ocean west to the Mississippi River. Cox calls West Florida—the land between the Mississippi and Apalachicola Rivers—a "residuary legatee of the international claims and controversies that hitherto characterized the history of the entire region."

My favorite part of that statement is how the strife over who could claim Florida is what defined the region. Forget oranges, forget sun-soaked beaches, forget magical springs that may or may not be the Fountain of Youth. When you said the word Florida in the late eighteenth century, people likely responded with, "Who's fighting over it *now?*" Which, if you think about it, is flattering, especially when you remember how much the rest of the country today loves to hate us. But for a few centuries, we were the hottest girl in town—every country wanted to take us to the prom. Put with slightly more sophistication, Florida, from 1513 to 1845, was a pawn in an international game of chess.

After Ponce de León, Pánfilo de Narváez and Hernando de Soto explored Florida on behalf of Spain. During the Age of Discovery, the lower half of North America was all considered part of the Spanish Empire, while Britain was content to travel to what we now call Canada. So there's plenty happening here before the British colonial period in North America, most of it Spanish. Which brings us to Florida and a man you've probably never heard of: Tristán de Luna y Arellano. In 1559, he tried to set up a cozy beach community in what we now call Pensacola, on present-day Florida's extreme western end. The outpost lasted until 1561. Nevertheless, it's the first European settlement in Florida to last more than a year in this New World. De Luna's travels before then had opened up the west side of Florida.

As Spain's trying to establish a stronghold in this New World, the French decide they want in on the fun, and Jean Ribault and René Goulaine de Laudonnière attempt, in 1564, to establish Fort Caroline in Jacksonville, thinking it will be a great place for Huguenot Protestants to flee from religious persecution. France sent six hundred colonists (they called them explorers) to help the three hundred Frenchmen who had tried to settle Fort Caroline the year before. But two days apart and just around the corner (literally; the two expeditions landed less than 50 miles apart) another made landfall on Florida's east coast. Pedro Menéndez de Avilés led six hundred Spaniards to St. Augustine with plans to evangelize the indigenous people, by force or reason. (Catholics historically have not been fussy as to one's motivation for conversion.)

The French knew the Spanish were there, and the Spanish knew the French were there. Things went poorly, and only when an oncoming hurricane shipwrecked Ribault and cloaked Menéndez's attack did the Spanish triumph. Had Ribault paid more attention to the weather, French-named forts and parks might pockmark Florida's east coast today. When Pedro Menéndez de Avilés destroys the settlement, it's a defining moment for the Spanish, because Menéndez founds St. Augustine, the oldest continuously operating settlement in the present-day United States established during colonial times.

So that's how Florida started, and while the Sunshine State did a phenomenal job of celebrating its five-hundredth birthday a few years back, it seems many folks have failed to wonder: If Florida is five hundred years old, what, exactly, were Floridians doing during the American Revolution? Why didn't they join the war to fight the Redcoats?

I am so glad you asked. The reason, unpalatable as it may be to our patriotic, *Hamilton*-loving hearts, is that not every colonist hated the British. Let's go back to St. Augustine in the seventeenth century. St. Augustine does quite well, growing to around two thousand settlers by the middle of the seventeenth century, all for the Spanish Crown. Then the Brits get into the action, and, starting in 1607 with the founding of Jamestown, they colonize the Atlantic Seaboard.

This is where the world stage starts to change Florida. Up until this point, we'd been happily Spanish (with that one minor skirmish with the French), but as British colonies grow in the rest of northeastern America, tensions between Spain and Britain grow, too. In brief, the British presence in North America started growing after the 1588 defeat of the Spanish Armada. That didn't spell the immediate end of the Spanish Empire, though. Spain kept control of Florida, but in 1739, England declares war on Spain, the latest in a series of conflicts known today as the Anglo-Spanish War. This had to do with places each wanted to rule across the globe, but in 1739, it played out in Florida. The British instruct General James Oglethorpe to pay special attention to St. Augustine, which he does.

Welcome to the War of Jenkins' Ear. In the eighteenth century, the newly founded Georgia is the popular girl at the dance; both Spain and England wanted to claim it. The Brits had the colonies to the north, and

Spain had Florida, which I think we can all agree was the better end of the deal, what with its beaches and better winters. Enter Robert Jenkins, with his two—at the time—perfectly serviceable ears. Jenkins, a smuggler loyal to the Brits, attempted to board a ship commanded by a Spanish privateer (that's what you call pirates when they're on your side). The privateer failed to appreciate Jenkins's zeal and cut off his ear, which of course the Brits took as an act of war (somehow, Jenkins kept the ear and took it back to Parliament instead of, oh, say, a board-certified surgeon). In short, a series of battles ensued in what we now call—with some degree of mirth—the War of Jenkins' Ear.

This is a delightful, macabre story, but odds are the ear part is at least partly made up. Let's think it through: How long would an ear have lasted on a ship in the 1730s? Long enough to get from present-day Georgia to England? Historians debate whether the ear made it back to England in any recognizable form, but one of the perhaps most deadpan discussion of these events comes not from those historians, but the researchers at the National Institutes of Health. Doctors authored a paper framing eighteenth-century ear repair techniques with the War of Jenkins' Ear. They describe parts of the attack better than anything else I've read:

"They motivated Jenkins' cooperation by hoisting him up the mast three times by a rope tied around his neck then casting him down the forward hatch"[1] and later "seized Jenkins, 'took hold of his left Ear, and with his Cutlass slit it down; and then another of the Spaniards took hold of it and tore it off, but gave him the Piece of his Ear again, bidding him carry it to his Majesty King George.'"[2] Now, they're quoting Ben Franklin's writing in the *Pennsylvania Gazette* in that last part, but they do note the eight-year difference between the Spanish cutting off part of Jenkins's ear (1731) and the British declaring the War of Jenkins' Ear (1739).[3]

Oglethorpe invaded Spanish Florida and attacked St. Augustine; the Spanish then attacked the British on St. Simon's Island. And so it went, back and forth, until, finally, with no clear winner and Jenkins's ear nothing but a disgusting lump of rotting flesh (if even that, at this point), Georgia went to the Brits, but Spain kept Florida.

The war, as you may surmise, wasn't really about the ear. It was about boundaries, and it was about Florida and Georgia. Whoever controlled peninsular Florida controlled shipping channels in the Caribbean, and, thus, the Caribbean. Florida was the prize, and the Spanish didn't want anyone else to get one inch closer to it.

Unfortunately for Spain, they sided with France in the French and Indian War (a.k.a. the Seven Years' War), and the British sided with the Indians (although both sides had such allies). When France lost, that meant Spain did, too, and in 1763, Spain had to give up Florida to the Brits if it wanted Havana back—which Spain did—and Britain split Florida in two, severing it at the Apalachicola to make it easier to govern.

East Florida ran from the Apalachicola east to the Atlantic Ocean, and south to the Florida Straits. West Florida ran west from the Apalachicola to the Mississippi River. Both Floridas had a northern edge of the 31st parallel, slightly north of Florida's present-day northern boundary. Think of these as the unsung fourteenth and fifteenth colonies. Kind of turns your grade-school perception of the colonies on its ear, doesn't it?

Which brings us to the American Revolution. When studying American history in high school—or even college—our teachers talk to us a lot about the colonies and the Revolutionary War. In Florida, somewhere in middle school, kids get a unit on Florida history. While I probably was not the best student, I don't remember hearing anything about us resisting the revolution, but that's what Florida did. We were a bunch of Tories down here—so much so, that many of the other colonists who wanted us to remain British fled to Florida.

Right, that's why we don't hear a lot about Florida during the Revolutionary War: although we'd only been British for thirteen years, unlike our thirteen brothers and sisters to the north, we didn't want a revolution. From our point of view, it wasn't a revolution; it was an insurrection, and we wanted no part of it. The only other British colonies that remained loyal to the Crown are now part of Canada—Nova Scotia and New Brunswick, Prince Edward Island, Newfoundland, and Quebec. Caribbean colonies also remained loyal—the Bahamas, the British Virgin Islands, Jamaica, and Bermuda are standouts. So we stayed loyal to Great Britain, and American historians essentially removed us from history until about 1822. But what did we do between the end of the American Revolution and that time? In 1783, Britain lost both Floridas *back* to Spain, which was a really lousy loyalty program for Floridian Tories.

Technically, Britain only had to cede East Florida, as the Spanish had already taken West Florida by force, with the 1781 capture of Pensacola.

For the rest of Florida's pre-US history, it remained two Spanish colonies, despite the best efforts of the young United States to take it over. And while Florida remains under Spanish control?

Well, that's where the pirates come in.

3

Key West

Pirates, Patriots, and Painters

Whether it's the ride or the movie, I've always been a sucker for pirates. Real pirates—not the ones wearing a ridiculous amount of clothing and rescuing swooning women—the ones who dealt with malaria and dysentery and, most likely, an inordinate amount of politics and red tape. And if you don't think of red tape when you think of pirates, you're only thinking of part of the story.

But let's back up. Or, actually, let's go forward—from the age of piracy to the Great Depression, during which the federal government paid writers to create a series of travel guides. In each state, the Federal Writers' Project paid writers with no jobs and no prospects to chronicle folklife and create driving tours of each state. The idea behind the guides was threefold: One, the government wanted to put people to work, even us writers; two, the guides would, in theory, get people to travel, at least locally; and three, the writers would capture a slice of life in pretty much every corner of America. Guide writers chronicled folklife and roadways in forty-eight states and Washington, DC. (Alaska and Hawaii were not yet states, although Guide writers did write about Alaska.) They also wrote about regions and cities. In addition to Florida's *Guide to the Southernmost State*, writers also wrote a separate book about Key West.

Here's the thing about Key West: it didn't get its own book because it was a tourist mecca, and it didn't become a tourist mecca for undergrads and various dropouts because of a boozy decadence that comes with being on the edge of America, where it feels like you're in another country, yet you're still protected by American laws. No, it took planning—and government assistance. That's right, Key West became a tourist destination because our federal government saw it as a way to save the small island.

Key West has a rich history of no small consequence. Florida became a state in 1845, but well before that, it played a pivotal role in US defense. To understand how a small outpost came to be habitable, let's look first at the island's physical attributes: limestone, saltwater, and sunshine. These are the three magic ingredients that make Key West a geographic constant. Along both Florida's coasts, barrier islands—made mostly of sand—offer the more traditional tropical respite, but they're ephemeral. Winds, currents, and hurricanes—most of all, hurricanes—rearrange our barrier islands periodically. Over time, Florida moves because of these shifting sands: as one side of the state erodes, the other side builds up barrier islands, which will eventually merge with the mainland.

Not so in the Keys, whose foundation rests on solid rock. This can be quite the disappointment to the sun-seeker arriving in the Keys hoping for a sandy beach. That's because ancient coral reefs in the Upper Keys and sandbars in the Lower Keys make up the limestone foundation. About 125,000 years ago, during the Pleistocene epoch, or the last ice age, sea levels dropped and exposed the reefs and sandbars—except by then, though, both the reefs and the sandbars had fossilized into this rock. It's not the marble and granite found in places north, but it's still rock, specifically, Key Largo limestone and Miami oolite.

Key West 100,000 years ago had a lot more land, and neighboring Florida Bay was a forest. Fun fact: Back then, the rich, swampy muck of the Everglades was a savanna, while the forests of Florida Bay, some historians suggest, resembled the Everglades we know today. Things pretty much stayed this way until a scant 15,000 years ago, when the glaciers started to melt. Parts of Key West and all of what is now Florida Bay flooded, leaving the nation's southernmost limestone rock. On that rock, a couple thousand years later, the people we would later call "Native Americans" would arrive. One theory suggests they arrived courtesy of a land bridge as wide as the distance from New York to Orlando, which suggests it wasn't so much a bridge as a vast isthmus. It started in Asia and ended in North America. However they arrived, though, the descendants of these folks would become the first northern transplants in the Florida Keys.

In breezy Euro-American style, we don't appear to care what these first Americans called themselves; instead, we focus on what we have called them. Some historians say Calusa lived in Key West; others claim it was the Tequesta. Some posit both. I suspect it was a faction of the same people, sometimes called (by Euro-Americans) the Matecumbe or the Guarungube. Whichever group it was: the fierce, reportedly wildly attractive Calusa, the first South Beach residents (sans the art deco) we know as the Tequesta, or the far-less-known Guarungube, one thing we do know: these people did not hunt big game. As the melting ice separated Key West from the rest of North America, so went big game. These tribes fished, and fished well.

This fishing culture continued until, on May 15, 1513, which happened to be the Day of the Feast of the Holy Spirit, Juan Ponce de León sailed by Key West, pausing long enough to give the island the name "Los Martires" (The Martyrs) because he believed the rocks rising from the sea looked like men who were suffering. He did not stop, but he identified the islands, and that was the first in a line of dominoes falling toward the Key West you see today.

William Whitehead, who surveyed Key West in 1829, talks of the time between Ponce de León's first "visit" (which, remember, wasn't a visit at all, but a sail-by) and the US' acquisition of the territory from Spain as almost a "dark age" for Key West, which is patently untrue. Tories, or British loyalists, headed for the Bahamas at the end of the war, in 1783, when Britain lost the Florida colonies but resumed control of the Bahamas. Coincidentally, the term for Key West residents, "Conchs," comes from migration patterns during this time. Cockney English who moved to the conch-laden Bahamas from England in 1649, seeking religious freedom, were known as the Eleutheran Adventurers. They later mixed with Tories who moved from Florida to the Bahamas when Spain regained control of the Tory-saturated Sunshine State in 1783. In the 1800s, their descendants migrated to Key West, hence the "Conch Republic."

Whitehead went on to say that during this time, Key West held little value for most: "The islands or keys were only resorted to by the aborigines of the country, the piratical crews with which the neighboring seas were infested, and fishermen."

Whitehead wrote of a tale he'd heard from an older settler, one who'd lived in southern Florida since 1775, that two Indian tribes lived along Florida's southern coast but were prone to fighting. These tribes swarmed south over the islands, fighting themselves and islanders as they went. Ultimately, they all landed on Key West, and a pre-prime-time version of *Survivor* ensued. The islanders, the third group and possibly the ones Euro-Americans would call "Guarungube," lost.

This is the battle, the settler told Whitehead, that covered Key West with bones, because the victors did not bother to bury the dead. From this bounty of bones came the island's name, Cayo Hueso, which, in Spanish, means Key of Bones. In time, Euro-Americans shortened "Hueso" to "west," and as the island is the farthest west, with the exception of the Dry Tortugas, it was easy for people to believe that was the origin of the name.

Shortly before Spain ceded Florida to the United States, the Spanish governor of Florida, Don Juan de Estrada, gave Cayo Hueso to a Spanish officer named Juan Pablo Salas, for services rendered without pay. Salas did nothing with the island until a year after it legally belonged to the United States, at which time he sold it to a man named John Simonton, a New Jersey native and Alabama merchant, for two thousand dollars. One problem with this deal, however: Salas had also made a conditional sale to a John Strong, who sold the island to John Geddes. This put a damper on Simonton's purchase, especially when Geddes sent a group to Key West on the US schooner *Revenge*. To settle the lawsuit that followed, Salas gave Geddes a boat and some acreage at Big Spring in East Florida. Remember, these sales both happened while Spain was selling Florida. The US Congress later said Simonton's claim to Key West was valid. Nevertheless, in 1822 the United States claimed its sovereignty over Key West, naming it "Thompson's Island." This name never caught on with the locals, who continued to call the island both Cayo Hueso and Key West. Whatever the locals called it didn't matter to the US Navy, who decided to use Key West as a base of operations to fight pirates in the West Indies.

The problem in fighting pirates—aside from the obvious ones—is that piracy isn't black-and-white. The word "pirates" covers a multitude of job descriptions. You may have heard of "privateers" or "profiteers," "marine salvagers" or "wreckers"; these are, depending on your definition (which also can change depending on which country you call home), all pirates. The Hollywood version of pirates, the rebels without a country, were not the order of the day in the Caribbean. In the case of the 1822 endeavor to rid the West Indies of pirates, the US used Key West as a home base to target pirates who just so happened to be working under the protection of Spain. Remember, Spain had *just* signed a treaty with the US to deed over Florida, and the Crown was less than amused by attacks on its sailors. It lodged a diplomatic protest when Commodore David Porter, whom the US Navy had tasked with leading the charge against these . . . sailors, captured the bulk of them in the area. The US court-martialed Porter and suspended him for six months, ultimately reassigning him to Turkey, where he died years later. He, too, had attempted to rename Key West—Allenton was his name of choice—but, as with Thompson's Island, the locals steadfastly refused to accept a new name.

Pirates or no pirates, people had started entrenching themselves in the lime rock of Key West. And even though they didn't call it piracy, many of the people who lived there made their living on a boat. Of course, history books now call it "salvaging wrecked vessels," but even those books admit there may have been a touch of "luring those ships onto reefs" so they would need saving.

Here's how wrecking worked: Say you're a merchant moving goods in a ship. Once you get within a few miles of Key West, if you don't know the waters, odds are, you're going to hit a reef. The best-case scenario if this happens is that you simply run aground without putting a hole in your ship's hull. The worst-case scenario is that you do rip a hole in your hull and the ship sinks.

Wreckers would come to your aid. By the mid-1830s Key West had at least twenty separate wreckers. The first wrecker to reach the distressed boat would win the rights to salvage. They'd get your crew to safety, and, if they could, they'd tow your ship or otherwise get it off the reef. If your ship was sinking, they'd salvage what they could before it did. Think of them as the SeaTow or TowBoat US of the nineteenth century. Except instead of you paying a three-hundred-dollar annual fee to them, they'd take their payment on the back end, and, once your ship was under their control (or at the bottom of the sea) and you, your crew, and any salvageable cargo were on one of their boats, you really had no room to negotiate, did you?

Jefferson Browne's 1912 book *Key West—The Old and the New* describes the wrecking process like this:

"A more thrilling site cannot be conceived than that of 20 or 30 sailing craft starting for a wreck. As if upon a preconcerted signal, sails would be hoisted, and as soon as jib and mainsail were up, moorings would be slipped and vessels got underway . . . the sight of these, dashing out of the harbor, with a stiff northeast wind, bunched together in groups of threes or fours, jibing with everything standing as they swung around the bend in the harbor off the foot of Duval Street was a scene never to be forgotten! No regatta could match it."

Bear in mind, no one considered this criminal. One master of a wrecking vessel was a parson who, upon sighting a wreck while preaching the Good Book, continued to preach as he walked down the aisle of the church. Just before he opened the church door, he called, "Wreck ashore!" and raced to his ship to beat his parishioners to the sinking ship.

In 1828, Congress set up a maritime jurisdiction court in Key West—not to stop the wrecking but to ensure that wrecking crews didn't take salvaged ships and booty to the Bahamas or Cuba. The court supervised the sale of wrecked ships and their cargo as well as the distribution of the proceeds. Bear in mind, the intention was not to ensure that the sailors who needed saving received a fair price; it was established to make sure the monies from the sale of salvaged goods were fairly distributed. Think of this as a pirate auction: people from across the United States would send their agents to bid on lace, liquor, and silver (to name a few) taken from wrecked vessels. Wrecking kept Key West afloat; if wreckers had a good year (meaning if the year had severe storms), receipts for wrecking could top $1.5 million. Translated into today's dollar, that's $33,374,994. For a population of 350 people, Key West's population in 1835, that's today's equivalent of a per-capita income of more than $95,000 per year, which made Key West, at that time, the wealthiest city in America.

Of course, all good things must come to an end, and by the middle of the nineteenth century, the government started installing reef lights, which signaled the beginning of the end for Key West's prosperity. Further national laws about who could operate a wrecker also narrowed the field.

As early as the 1820s, with its antipiracy campaign, the military recognized the strategic significance of Key West. In the 1830s, the US Army established a post in Key West, and for the next several decades the government made military fortifications to the island. These fortifications include Fort Taylor and the two Martello Towers. In the latter half of the 1850s, the US Navy also made its way to Key West. During the Civil War, Monroe County continued to fly the US flag rather than a Confederate one. This was in no small part credited to the large US Army and Navy presence in Key West. Anecdotal evidence suggests citizens sympathized with the Confederacy, and only after federal authorities issued orders prohibiting flying Confederate flags did those flags come down from several buildings. A local paper, *Key of the Gulf*, published strong arguments favoring secession until the government suppressed it in 1861. Key West's military allegiance with the Union likely played a huge factor in the Union's victory. During the war, the US Navy captured 299 blockade-runners attempting to assist the Confederacy.

So, while Florida seceded from the Union, the Union never relinquished Key West. Union troops moved into Fort Taylor, on which work had started in 1845 but didn't finish until the North took possession. The Union expected the townspeople would attack the fort (which they never did) and ordered anyone who had spoken a word of disloyalty deported to Port Royal, South Carolina. This did not please the townspeople, to the point where Union sympathizers and secessionists joined in protest. It was the Union sympathizers who sent a protest to Washington, and on the day boats filled with six hundred Conchs were to leave Key West, a former commanding officer, Colonel Good, suspended the order. The mainland and its problems, despite what must have been an overwhelming military occupation, still seemed, it appears, quite removed from the day-to-day lives of the Conchs. During Reconstruction, much remained as it was in Key West. The military never left, not really, and today the Conchs are used to the presence. More of a force than Reconstruction was Cuba.

In 1868, Cuba proclaimed its independence from Spain, although things really weren't that straightforward. Carlos Manuel de Céspedes led the movement for Cuban independence. What ensued was a ten-year war, called Guerra de los Diez Años. During this time Cubans arrived in Key West in earnest. Cigar companies built factories in Key West, often supplying their own workers, who, of course, brought their own families. With that many Cubans out from under the Spanish thumb, it was only a matter of time before Cubanos began plotting to overthrow the Spanish government. José Martí, along with other Cuban leaders, visited Key West.

That same year, Vicente Martinez Ybor moved his cigar factory to Key West. Within a few years, Key West was said to produce 100 million cigars annually. In 1886, a fire blazed for twelve hours and destroyed an estimated half of the city, including Ybor's cigar factories, which he rebuilt near Tampa Bay. This destruction resulted in no small part from the city's steam engine being inauspiciously in New York, getting repaired. Property loss totaled $2 million. The city rebuilt, and, in a boost to the city's recovery, the Peninsular and Occidental Steamship Company started biweekly trips between Key West and Tampa. It is during this time we see mule-drawn streetcars, the availability of utilities such as gas and electric, and an ice plant.

The Flagler Railroad truly changed life in not just Key West, but the Florida Keys. Henry Flagler had, in today's money, roughly nine gazillion dollars. He earned that money as one of the partners, along with John D. Rockefeller, in Standard Oil. There's more about the railroad in the next chapter, but for the purposes of this one, we're fast-forwarding to the 1920s, as Flagler's Extension continued, a vital link between New York and Havana. Passengers traveled the rail line, and so, oddly enough, did pineapples. The Upper Keys at this time had a glut of pineapple plantations, and by 1924, 3,500 train cars of pineapples passed through Key West every year—in a period of six weeks. Days on which pineapples arrived were known as "pineapple days." Key West also sent passels of hogs to Cuba, and they kept those hogs penned at Trumbo Island.

During Prohibition, the railroad helped keep Key West "open," because Key West never truly went dry—Cuba was too close, and it was too easy to get rum. Never proven was the speculation that sealed coffins coming from Cuba with the cause of death listed as "alcoholism" were, in fact, filled with bootleg rum. Islanders could find the rum through a variety of sources, but one creative way was to look for signs hidden in plain sight. You could find many things in Key West by looking for what wasn't there—if the negative space in the gingerbread trim shaped a bottle, people knew they could get alcohol inside, such as was the case with Tampa native Raul Vasquez's home on Duval, today called the Speakeasy Inn.

Just after Prohibition ended in the US, however, something else interrupted the steady flow of rum between Cuba and Key West: the weather.

The death knell for the Key West Extension was the Hurricane of 1935. On Labor Day of 1935, a Category 5 hurricane swept through the Keys and killed 408 people. It was said the force of the wind blew the sand with such force it stripped the clothes off people standing out in the open. The maximum recorded wind was 160 miles per hour. It destroyed large portions of the track, and the monies received for hurricane-related damage—$640,000—wouldn't cover the cost of one bridge.

Because the Overseas Extension was exclusively a private endeavor, an exact accounting of construction costs has never been made available to historians. However, a 1916 estimate suggests Flagler spent $27,280,000 building the railroad. That's more than $575 million in today's money.

Although Flagler had left money to sustain and, if needed, rebuild the railroad, the line had gone into receivership as depression swept across the nation. Historians tend to blame mismanagement; the men who had poured their hearts and souls into the line had started to die, and those replacing them lacked the passion of their predecessors. Today, the Overseas Highway runs the path the railroad once followed.

The Great Depression played no small part in the shuttering of the Over-the-Sea Railroad. Fortunately, the city's rebirth was about a year under way when the hurricane decimated the railroad.

In the 1830s, Key West was the wealthiest city in America; a century later, that city was bankrupt. The railroad's destruction all but destroyed the fishing and shipping industries, and the days of the wrecker or the pirate or the privateer were long gone. This was not an "on paper" bankruptcy: the city had no money to pay its employees. Eighty percent of residents received some form of federal assistance. In July 1934, the city council passed a petition asking Florida governor Dave Sholtz to declare a state of emergency in Key West. Governor Sholtz authorized the Federal Emergency Relief Administration to begin rehabilitating the city's economy.

This is how Key West became the city we know today: government relief. Because Key West asked for help, the help it got was not the garden-variety Works Progress Administration (WPA) help that built bridges or roads.

No, our government decided what Key West needed was tourists. The plan? Make Key West a tourist destination on par with Bermuda and Nassau, only stateside, so people wouldn't have to get on a boat or plane (unless they wanted to) and go to another country.

How do you make a tourist destination out of the hottest, most isolated town in America when there isn't a sandy beach anywhere in sight? Marketing and grunt labor. Conchs volunteered more than 2 million hours of their time doing everything from cleaning streets to making beaches. They also helped build a sanitation system and renovate and redecorate houses. Hotels that hadn't been in business for years got reopened, and festivals were created specifically to draw tourists. One such festival, a weeklong celebration of the dramatic and choral arts, culminated with a production of *Pirates of Penzance*.

While the WPA and Key West did a fantastic job promoting this island of the arts, there was one small problem: it *wasn't* an island of the arts. It was a city filled with fishermen and the descendants of shipwreck survivors and pirates and great-grandchildren of Bahamian refugees, but artists? Not so much. Fortunately for Key West, artists were as broke as the rest of the United States during the Great Depression, and it was no problem to find an artist receiving relief. Julius Stone, the administrator of the Federal Emergency Relief Administration, decided to simply import artists of all sorts to fill Key West with art. Some of those artists created works of art that would promote Key West as a tourist destination, such as postcards, travel brochures, and guidebook illustrations. Stone brought in still other artists to paint murals and create engravings on copper and paintings depicting island life. Out-of-work writers were brought in to write brochure copy designed to entice visitors who stopped over en route to the Bahamas. The government shipped in performers to present operas and pageants.

Whatever talent the government could not import, it created. Remember that 80 percent receiving federal assistance? As part of FDR's New Deal, they received training in making art. Some of the art was traditional, such as drawings, while other art was more, shall we say, commercially oriented. Conchs learned to make ashtrays, buttons, buckles and pins from coconuts, hats, purses, and rugs from palm fiber, and assorted novelties from fish scales and seashells.

To further entice visitors to stay, the government established a housing service that not only provided lodging but hired servants and stocked the pantry.

Across the nation, city planners lauded this bold community-planning experiment. No one had attempted anything like this. And it worked. It was the last major change the island would see; it remains, today, a tourist mecca, the end of the line for weary travelers and hopeful new residents.

And yet, tourism of the island has changed, although some of the WPA's Key West guidebook's thirty-one points of interest remain.

In what seems perhaps the oddest juxtaposition of drunken debauchery and culture, the San Carlos Institute still lives on Duval Street, a two-story tribute to the Cuban patriot Carlos Manuel de Céspedes—

remember, he came here and led the movement for Cuban independence from Spain. Founded in 1871, the museum once held the Cuban consul and an opera house. Today it serves many purposes, including museum, art gallery, theater, and school.

Down the road is the Watlington House, the oldest house in Key West. It was built in 1825 and, as with the San Carlos, still stands on Duval Street and offers tours. Duval Street is not its original location; the house was built by a Captain Cousins on Whitehead Street and moved to Duval in 1832. The cedar in the home reportedly comes from Cuba. Captain Cousins sold it to Francis Watlington, a boat captain who ran a schooner between the Dry Tortugas, Key West, and Cuba.

The Bahama Houses are private homes on the southwest corner of Eaton and Williams Streets. A thick fringe of trees shields the homes from passersby, but the homes—built in the Bahamas—still stand. When the families moved to Key West, they took apart the houses, loaded them on schooners, brought them to Key West, and rebuilt them.

The guidebook mentions, too, the cemetery, and while there's no denying the historical significance of this expansive cemetery, which has one section devoted to soldiers who lost their lives on the USS *Maine* and another for Cuban patriots who died in the Spanish-American War, one of the fun things about it is looking at the headstones, which seem to have a Key West sense of humor. My favorite? The grave of B. P. Roberts, whose epitaph reads only: "I told you I was sick."

Rest Beach, today called Higgs Beach, is east of West Martello Tower. In 1860, American ships carrying Africans to Cuba to be sold into slavery were intercepted by the US Navy. The men, women and children were brought to Key West. Some were healthy enough to return to Africa, but 294 died in Key West. They are buried on Rest Beach by the tower.

The Pan-American airfield, now the Key West International Airport, has the distinction of being the site of the first international flight in the United States. A plane took off here and landed in Havana. The international flight was all of 90 miles, but still, Key West counts it.

Finally, along with the San Carlos Institute, the Key West Art Center is one of the few places mentioned in the 1941 *Guide to Key West* that still exists in its original iteration. It's in the same place, with a gallery on the second floor. The center operates as a nonprofit and still offers lectures and art shows.

That's not all there is to Key West, of course. I've not discussed the federal blockade that led to the city seceding from the US in 1982, and I have not mentioned Jimmy Buffett once. It is not because these parts of the city's history don't matter; it's because stories of "Key Weird" often overshadow the island's rich history.

To so many visitors, Duval Street is a place to get drunk and buy a T-shirt, but they walk past the San Carlos Institute, the Watlington House, or where the former library once stood. I'm not saying you shouldn't have a drink in Key West, or seven or eight, if that's what you wish. I'm saying that if you go there, you should know that every dollar you spend is part of a ninety-year-old government plan to get you to have that drink, buy that T-shirt, and disappear, for a while, into a place inhabited by pirates, patriots, and painters.

4

Frenemies

Florida's Two Henrys

The story of Key West, of course, must include the story of the railroad in Key West, and the story of the railroad in Key West isn't simply the story of the railroad in Key West, but the story of the railroad in Florida, and I can't tell *that* story without telling the story of two frenemies.

Most women I know—and a few men—have *that* friend. The frenemy. A frenemy is a person you consider a friend—sort of. You get along well enough, on the surface, but underneath, there's either a good bit of dislike or a healthy rivalry.

Henry Plant and Henry Flagler were exactly that: friendly rivals, or frenemies. And that frenemy-ship—that's not really a word, I don't think, but I don't know what else to call it—helped Florida become what it is today, both good and bad.

The two men had quite a bit in common. They were both born in the 1800s, they both married more than once, they both had more money than we'll ever hope to see (and if any of you can argue with that last statement, I'd like to talk to you about funding me as a full-time novelist), and they both built railroads.

Our two Henry lived in a different time, when America had a ruling wealthy class but not much of a middle class. These two men belonged to that wealthy ruling class. And it wasn't a big group, so they not only knew *of* one another, they knew each other. And they had similar interests that would make them more wealthy, and so, as they pursued those interests—and decided to pursue them in Florida, which was open for exploitation—they developed a passive-aggressive sort of friendship, a rivalry from which we've all benefited. Because they had the means to "go big or go home," they competed using Florida as a battlefield, and because of that, Florida changed forever.

Let's break that down.

Henry Plant was born in Branford, Connecticut, in 1819; Henry Flagler came into the world eleven years later, in 1830, almost eighty miles away in Hopewell, New York. Plant married twice; Flagler took three wives. Both men came to Florida on a doctor's suggestion, to improve the health of their ailing first wives, because apparently that was a cure-all in the nineteenth century: Go to Florida! Both wives ultimately died, Ellen Blackstone eight years after Plant came to Florida and Mary Harkness three years after coming to Florida. Both men became millionaires before Congress passed the Sixteenth Amendment in 1909 (it was ratified in 1913). The Sixteenth Amendment allows for a federal income tax, which some have argued makes it almost impossible for people to gain the type of wealth both Henrys had.

How wealthy were they? Well, at the time of his death, Flagler's net worth was $60 million, or $1.6 billion in 2021 dollars. Plant "only" had $17 million when he died in 1899. To put that in perspective, in 2015, Donald Trump's net worth was $3.7 billion, or about twice Plant's wealth. That kind of kills the argument that income tax makes great wealth impossible, but "tax code and billionaires" is probably another chapter or book in its own right, and one I have no desire to write. Let's get back to our two Henrys and, of course, how they came to Florida.

Other than crazy amounts of money and wives in poor health, what common thread ran through both of these men's lives? Trains. Well, technically, railroads. Railroads, and also hotels and steamship companies. Both men lined the coasts of Florida with railroads and, along different rail stops, they built these breathtakingly luxe hotels. This was during the Gilded Age, which started in 1878 and lasted until 1889. During the Gilded Age, immigrants provided cheap labor for mining gold and silver, and they also worked turning trees into lumber. Iron and steel production also increased dramatically. The gold, silver and lumber available in the West made it necessary to transport those resources back to the factories and banking centers in the East, and so the country found itself quite badly in need of ways to transport raw materials cheaply and relatively quickly. That meant there was a grand opportunity for someone to build that transportation.

Enter our two Henrys and their northern railroads, because that's where their frenemy-ship begins.

Henry Flagler worked in a grain store as a teenager. As an adult, he and his half brother Dan founded D. M. Harkness and Company, and Flagler married Mary Harkness, Dan's half sister. (While Dan and Flagler had the same mother, they had different fathers, and Dan's father also had a daughter, Mary.) In 1862 he and his brother-in-law, whose last name was York, founded the Flagler and York Salt Company. The Union was using an incredible amount of salt during the war, as a preservative—after all, things do spoil more quickly in the South—and so the company did quite well.

Quite well, that is, until the war ended and no one needed an awful lot of salt all the time, and the company collapsed. Flagler lost not only his own investment in the company, which was $50,000, but the $30,000 his half brother and his father-in-law had loaned him, which had to make for an awkward Thanksgiving dinner. However, he went back to the grain business and a commission merchant and paid back the money within the year, which is probably why when he asked to borrow $100,000 from another relative to start a new company with an acquaintance, that relative agreed to loan him the money with the condition he be made 25 percent owner in the company. That acquaintance?

John D. Rockefeller. The company? Standard Oil. This is where Flagler's money troubles pretty much ended forever.

Money, however, can't buy everything, and Flagler's wife suffered ill health. In 1878, her doctor suggested taking her south, and the Flaglers went to Jacksonville. In 1881, his wife died. In 1883, Flagler remarries, to Ida Alice Shourds, and they travel to St. Augustine, where Flagler smelled opportunity, because he and his new bride couldn't find a decent place to stay or decent transportation.

So bothered by the lack of a convenient Uber or the availability of a Holiday Inn was Flagler that he surrendered his day-to-day responsibilities at Standard Oil and bought the Jacksonville, St. Augustine, & Halifax River Railroad—the line ran between Jacksonville and St. Augustine—in 1885. Jacksonville, a major shipping depot and deepwater port, already had a railroad, but it didn't connect to the coast. Halifax connected these two cities, but Flagler took it one step further: he used his new purchase to offer 30-hour Pullman sleeping car service to New

York City, which turned St. Augustine into a winter destination. He re-named the line the Jacksonville, St. Augustine & Indian River Railway. From there, he wanted to go south. When he arrived in Miami on April 15, 1896, he renamed the railroad the Florida East Coast Railway System.

While Florida had Henry Flagler on the East Coast, we cannot ignore Henry Plant running rail line down the West.

Plant, unlike Flagler, didn't go broke at the end of the Civil War; he benefited from it. He'd worked on steamships, but when he married in 1843, he decided to stick closer to home and took a job with Beecher and Company, where they transferred him from steamers to railroads. Adams Express Company took over Beecher, and Plant rose through the ranks. His wife, though, became ill, and her doctor ordered her to a warmer climate, again, because healthcare for ladies in the nineteenth century left a lot to be desired. The Plants wintered in Jacksonville, and Plant saw opportunity; when his wife's doctor ordered her back south for her health the following year, he asked for—and received—responsibility for the company's interests in areas south of the Potomac and Ohio Rivers. With this new area of charge, he extended express service across the South.

As the idea of a war between the states loomed closer, the company, by that time called the Adams Express Company, feared the government confiscation of their properties in the Deep South, so they agreed to sell them to Plant for a half million dollars. Along with southern stockholders, he founded the Southern Express Company in 1861. When the Civil War came to pass, the cabinet of the Confederate States of America president, Jefferson Davis, made Southern Express the agent for the Confederacy to collect tariffs and transfer funds. In 1863, Plant claimed he was gravely ill and left his home in Augusta with a "safe passage" document signed by Davis. He sailed to Bermuda, spent a month there, and then went to Canada, Connecticut, England, and France, where he learned his Confederate passport was not valid. This was not a typical thing to do, but French authorities issued him a French passport declaring him a US citizen who lived in Georgia; this allowed him to travel and later return to New York through Canada.

Plant returned to the South in 1865, after the Civil War, and that's when he really made his mark—the southern railroads were all but ruined, because the Union wanted to cut any way to get supplies to Confederate soldiers, and by destroying the railroads and taking control of the ports, they did exactly that. Many railroads went bankrupt during Reconstruction, and Plant wasted no time buying a number of railroads in the former Confederate states, because he believed the South would once again flourish. He bought the Atlantic and Gulf Railroad and the Charleston and Savannah Railroad, both in foreclosure, and used them as building blocks to create a transportation system that, within two decades, would include fourteen railway companies, 2,100 miles of track, several steamer lines, and hotels.

In 1882 Plant, with help from northern capitalists, including Henry Flagler, formed the Plant Investment Company, a holding company that would manage various properties under his control. He rebuilt and extended several small railroads to allow for continuous service across Florida and, because the Plant System of Railroads could get their products easily north, he gave Florida's orange growers quick, inexpensive access to northern markets. So, if you grew up drinking orange juice for breakfast and you didn't grow up in Florida, you can thank Henry Plant. This consolidated railway went on to become the Atlantic Coast Line Railroad, which, today, is a major part of Florida's CSX Transportation.

So that's how the railroads came to Florida, but without the next part of the equation, it would have been of no use to bring people on those railroads, because the places to stay? We didn't have so many of those. Our two Henrys, though, were about to change that.

Let's start with Flagler, because he beat his buddy Henry Plant to the punch. Flagler was no millionaire by accident; he knew if he brought people down on his railroads and gave them a place to stay, he'd have a corner on the market. And so, as he built the railroad in Florida, he built hotels close to the stations. In St. Augustine, he ultimately had three.

Perhaps the best-known hotel in St. Augustine was—and is—the Ponce de Leon. Work on "the Ponce" began December 1, 1885. On January 10, 1888, the Ponce de Leon hotel opened. Flagler hired two promising young architects from the well-known firm McKim, Mead & White. This launched their careers; with their design for the Ponce, John Carrere and Thomas Hastings launched a new architectural firm, Carrere & Hastings, which went on to gain national prominence.

Flagler chose the Spanish Renaissance Revival style for the design because he wanted the hotel to "match" St. Augustine's historic Spanish settings. He asked Louis C. Tiffany to design the inside, and design he did—using stained glass, mosaics, and terra-cotta relief on the walls and ceilings. Tiffany commissioned several grand murals. The structure itself has architectural significance—it was the first large-scale building constructed entirely of poured concrete. This hotel's popularity didn't stop in St. Augustine; it impacted southern Florida architecture for at least the next fifty years.

The hotel had 450 rooms, called apartments, steam heat, which didn't get much use, and electric lights in every room, which were a novelty. Electric lights were so uncommon at the time that the hotel had to hire extra staff, because many guests feared getting shocked by turning lights on and off. So, yes, the Ponce had staff whose sole purpose was turning lights on and off for guests.

Unfortunately, the hotel's success can best be described as "episodic"— pre–World War II Florida was tough going, even for guests at an opulent resort. As soon as Flagler opened the Ponce, a yellow fever epidemic swept the area. In late 1894 and early 1895, Florida had the worst freezes in its history, which is not really the headline you want when you're marketing a warm, sunny winter resort.

But, see, that was the problem—St. Augustine *wasn't* as warm and sunny as other parts of Florida, and as Flagler extended his railroad south, he opened *other* opulent resorts, so people went to those instead. While St. Augustine never grew into a booming winter resort town, tourists *did* go there and the Ponce de Leon was one of only four Flagler Hotels to survive the Great Depression. After World War II, although tourism had declined, the hotel still attracted large enough crowds to survive, but by the mid-1960s the appeal of the hotel declined enough that the Ponce closed. Flagler College bought it that same year; they've renovated it, and it looks much like it must have when Flagler built it.

This next part is what historians like to call "anecdotal history," which means we can't prove it's true, but gosh, it makes a good story. Supposedly, when Plant finished building the Tampa Bay Hotel in 1891, he had a custom-engraved invitation for the opening ball sent to Flagler. Flagler allegedly sent him a telegraph back that read "Invitation received. Where the hell is the Tampa Bay Hotel?" According to the story, Mr. Plant telegraphed back, "just follow the crowds."

Sometimes this story gets told in reverse, with Flagler inviting Plant to the opening of the Royal Palm Hotel on the Miami River in 1896, with the same snarky discourse.

When Plant was building his railroad empire, he made choices that changed Florida in ways we don't even think about anymore. Take the Tampa Bay Hotel: it was along Plant's railroad, and Tampa, to our modern brains, makes sense for its location. After all, the port of Tampa is here, and it's a fairly populated area. But that's not why Plant chose it; he built the railroad into Tampa, and when he did, he damned another city: Cedar Key.

Cedar Key had a port, a significant one, that shipped lumber and naval stores, which is what we called turpentine and other pine tree products. Cedar Key also produced cedar slats that would get shipped north and become pencils. It had a lighthouse and, in 1860, was the terminus for the Florida Railroad, Florida's first cross-state railroad, connecting Cedar Key to Fernandina on Florida's east coast. On March 1, 1861, the first train arrived in Cedar Key, only weeks before the Civil War started. During the war, Union Soldiers tore up thirty miles of track and Confederate soldiers salvaged parts of the railroad to build a new railroad. With the railroad rebuilt, things looked good for the bustling port city—until Henry Plant took his railroad to Tampa. This delivered a crushing blow to the economy of Cedar Key, and when the final storm of the 1896 hurricane season covered the island with a ten-foot storm surge, one hundred people died. Cedar Key turned to the sea for its economy, and today it's known for its multimillion-dollar clam industry, which it would not have, had it grown to be the bustling city Tampa is today. Tampa's place as Florida's third-largest city is thanks largely to Plant. His Tampa Bay Hotel cost more than $3 million to build, or roughly $80 million in today's money. People called it "Plant's folly"—Tampa had almost no people, and it was a hot, wet swamp. But Plant persisted. He made no secret he wanted his hotel to compete with Flagler's, so he made sure to include a golf course, tennis courts, boathouse, and a horse racing track. His hotel had silver minarets and a huge porch; he and his wife traveled Europe, filling thirty railcars with art and furnishings. Plant built a power station on the grounds to provide electricity to the hotel. He also built a 2,000-seat performing arts center/casino (not a gambling venue, but recreation hall) with a floor that could roll away so people could use a 50-by-70-foot swimming pool. The hotel had 500 rooms, was five stories tall, and sat alongside the Hillsborough River. The railroad continued on another ten miles to the port, which, years later, was dredged to allow better shipping. The Tampa Bay Hotel opened on February 5, 1891, and operated past Plant's death; the City of Tampa bought it in 1905 for a paltry $100,000; the hotel closed during the Great Depression. Since 1933, the University of Tampa has used it, and today the building houses the Plant Museum. By the 1930s, "Plant's folly" had a value of more than $5 million, or almost $72 million today.

Back in St. Augustine, in 1889, Flagler opened the Alcazar, which also had a casino. The Alcazar also had a 120-foot-long pool, fed by an artesian well. He used the same architect who designed the Hotel Ponce de Leon and, later, the Whitehall, Flagler's Palm Beach home. This hotel's popularity peaked in the 1890s, when more than twenty-five thousand guests visited and many others took advantage of that casino—along with what was, at the time, the largest indoor swimming pool in the country, the grand ballroom, sulfur baths, a steam room, massage parlor, gymnasium, bowling alley, archery ranges, tennis courts, and a bicycle academy. Hotel Alcazar now serves as perhaps the fanciest city hall in the United States. It's also home to the Lightner Museum, which has collections of nineteenth-century fine and decorative art.

In 1887, Plant built the PICO (which stood for Plant Investment Company) Hotel in Sanford. It had Moorish and Romanesque Revival styles. This hotel had the Turkish dome not unlike the ones on the Tampa Bay Hotel, but it was destroyed in a storm in the 1950s.

On the East Coast, Flagler acquired St. Augustine's Casa Monica. He didn't build this hotel; Franklin W. Smith, a man who was instrumental in getting Flagler to invest in Florida, did. Smith, known as a Victorian architecture enthusiast, built this hotel in 1888 and followed Flagler's lead, using poured concrete and leaving the exterior walls with a natural finish, which kept the building looking like the other buildings of the time—including ones Flagler built. The Casa Monica mixed Moorish Revival and Spanish Baroque styles. Shortly after he finished building it, Smith ran into financial trouble and sold the hotel and everything in it to Flagler for $325,000. Flagler renamed it the Cordova and used it for balls, charity events, and other functions until 1902.

In 1902, a bridge stretched over Cordova Street, providing a pedestrian walkway to the Hotel Alcazar. The Cordova became the Alcazar Annex, which is not nearly as glamorous a name.

At this point in the story, Flagler decided to push south, as did Henry Plant. The Tampa Bay Hotel gets all the attention, but Plant built another hotel in Tampa—the Port Tampa Inn, built in 1888. Port Tampa is near MacDill, south of Gandy, and the area has changed but still exists. It was settled in 1885, through the efforts of Henry Plant. This hotel was not as opulent—guests could get off the train, step over to their hotel and fish off their porch, or step onto a steamship that, coincidentally, Plant also owned. Port Tampa, thanks to Plant's effort, played a part in the Spanish-American War—Teddy Roosevelt and his Rough Riders passed through here; it was their point of departure for the war. That's because Plant lobbied like crazy to get the War Department to select Tampa as an assembly point. In April 1898, the War Department agreed. This little city—it was incorporated in 1893—put Tampa on the map.

Oh, and those steamships? Guess who owned them? Yup, Henry Plant. So you took his railroad to your hotel, which he owned, then you stepped onto a steamship, which he also owned. He wasn't heading aggressively south like Flagler was with his railroad, but he was creating a sort of monopoly wherever passengers stepped off his trains.

Flagler bought the Hotel Ormond in 1890. Nearby auto races attracted visitors (Ormond Beach is quite close to Daytona). Flagler's former partner—and longtime friend—Rockefeller built a house across the street from the hotel. Flagler's Jacksonville hotel opened in 1901 and only served summer tourists; its season ran from late March through August.

Plant built the Seminole Hotel in Winter Park in 1891; in 1894, Flagler opened the Hotel Royal Poinciana in Palm Beach. This hotel had indoor plumbing, electricity, and telephones, and, in 1905, was the world's largest hotel and also the world's largest wooden structure. The hotel was demolished in 1936, making Plant's Belleview Biltmore, just south of Clearwater, the largest wooden structure in the world. Plant had started work on the Biltmore in 1896, but work didn't finish until after he died. It had 400,000 square feet and a moat, casino, two golf courses, a riding stable, and a spur connecting private cars to the Plant System; this line was called the Pinellas Special.

There's another great story that, once again, is anecdotal but has a grain of fact. Supposedly, Plant's son was badly injured in a car crash while at the Biltmore, but there were no decent medical facilities in the area. The family, fortunately, had the railroad at its disposal and ordered three railcars filled with supplies and personnel rushed to the area. Plant's son lived and those three railcars became the foundation of a hospital not so far from the Biltmore. Morton Plant Hospital has perhaps the best water views of all Florida hospitals, as it overlooks the bay from a bluff not so far from the site of the Biltmore. It was the last of Plant's eight hotels, in operation until 2009, when it closed. From there, it suffered "demolition by neglect" and was demolished almost entirely in the second decade of the millennium. New owners have preserved a small section of the building, but the grandeur of the wooden hotel is long gone.

Flagler opened the Palm Beach Inn in 1896; this was his second hotel in Palm Beach, and today we know it as the Breakers. Initially, he intended it as an overflow hotel but quickly realized tourists preferred this hotel on the beach. In 1903 it had a fire, which destroyed it, and Flagler rebuilt it; that's when he changed the name to the Breakers. In 1925 the Breakers had another fire that destroyed the hotel again, but Flagler's family rebuilt it in eleven months, reopening in 1926. This time, they wanted to honor Flagler's vision and what had been an unassuming hotel became what we know today; architects drew inspiration from Rome's Villa Medici. The Breakers still stands today in all its Flagler glory.

Flagler originally planned to retire in Palm Beach, but the winter of 1894–95 freeze convinced him if he brought the railroad farther south, it would one day have access to America's winter crops. A long accepted but wholly debunked story involves Julia D. Tuttle, the founder of Miami and also the only woman to found an American city.

This urban legend says she sent Flagler a blossoming orange branch in the midst of the freeze and that lured him to the south. In reality, Flagler had his eye on a bigger prize than the nascent Miami, and he was no doubt watching his "frenemy" race down the west coast of Florida—Plant had built the Hotel Punta Gorda in Punta Gorda in 1894—so Flagler went full steam ahead. He opened this hotel in 1897, in a town called Fort Dallas. It shared features with the Royal Poinciana, and residents wanted to rename the town for him, but he instead suggested naming the town for a local river, which they did. The Hotel Royal Palm quickly became the top resort in . . . Miami.

When Flagler's train reached Miami in 1896, hundreds of eager settlers had already sailed into Lemon City, which was the only developed port in Biscayne Bay. New Miami residents greeted the railroad.

Plant built the Ocala House in Ocala in 1895, at the time the largest brick hotel in the state. Three years later, he built the Fort Myers Hotel in Fort Myers. There, he stopped.

Flagler, however, was not to be stopped at Miami simply because the formal edge of North America's east coast ended there. Remember, the Miami we know today has been dredged out of a swamp. It isn't high-and-dry land. Getting the railroad to that point was no small task. Extending it farther would involve an undertaking never before seen in North America.

In 1904, shortly after the United States started working on the Panama Canal, Flagler decided it was time to bring his railroad to sea. Realizing the value a railroad could have if it ran to the deepwater US port closest to the canal, Flagler intended to extend the railroad to Cape Sable, at the western edge of the Everglades, but, for several reasons, building a railroad across the Glades was not possible. Instead, Flagler chose Key West.

Work on the Oversea (sometimes called Over-the-Sea) Railroad began in 1904.

By 1912, Flagler's workers completed the railroad to Key West, without the assistance of government; it was a wholly private undertaking to run 156 miles of track to Key West. Workers had toiled in both Key West and Miami. Trains would have to span many channels, including what we know as the Seven Mile Bridge. Today, as you motor south to Key West over the Seven Mile Bridge, you can see the remnants of the railroad to your west and imagine what an adventure such a train ride would have been—at the midpoint of the channel, you can barely see land, just turquoise water everywhere.

As work continued in between storms and various tragedies, Flagler's health began to fail. Rumors that only his desire to ride a train into Key West were keeping him alive. He was eighty-one years old when his chief of construction received a request to finish the railroad so that, on Flagler's next birthday—January 2, 1912—he could arrive in Key West by train. The chief of construction replied that he could shave a year off construction, but that would still put the railroad's completion slightly after Flagler's eighty-second birthday.

His advancing age did not dull his mind. When Flagler was told there wasn't enough land to build a rail terminal on Key West, he calmly told workers, "then make some." To do just that, an engineer named Howard

Trumbo joined the project. Key West was not always quite as expansive—if you can call it that—as it is today. Trumbo dredged 134 acres of land on the northwest side of the island, drawing protests from the US Navy that he was using mud for fill that it may need one day. His response? If that happened, Trumbo said, he would give the mud back. Today, the entirety of Trumbo Island, the name for the terminal, belongs to the US Navy. The Trumbo Island terminal had a 1,700-foot-long by 134-foot-wide pier that allowed train passengers to step off a train and, not more than a few feet away, board a steamship for Havana. The trains would pull up alongside the boats.

On January 22, 1912, the Extension Special pulled into Key West carrying, among others, Henry Flagler in his private car, called *Rambler*. His car had a copper-lined shower, a kitchen with a coal stove, guest quarters, and an oak-paneled lounge. Also on board that day was William Howard Taft's assistant secretary of war and a number of Latin American dignitaries. While the idea of a railroad in Florida had started as one to get visitors to his grand resorts, Flagler did not make an astonishing amount of money by ignoring opportunity, and the potential for shipping from Key West to the Panama Canal was of great interest to all those on board. The extension was hailed as the "Eighth Wonder of the World."

Flagler pulled into Trumbo Island, where a three-day party awaited him. Schoolchildren threw flowers in his path and sang him songs, although he was too blind to see them. The Key West mayor spoke; ships in the harbor blew their whistles. A band played.

"Now," he said, "I can die in peace." His calculations, however, were slightly off, and he lived for another sixteen months.

These two incredible men did a lot for Florida. Certainly, they had their faults. They were products of their times; in his book *Last Train to Paradise*, Les Standiford makes the point that Flagler's Key West Extension wouldn't have been possible with modern environmental sensibilities and laws.

No doubt both men destroyed precious parts of Florida as they laid a track to a better tomorrow, and certainly they wouldn't have thought twice about whether they displaced any Seminole Indians. To call them "products of a different time" does not excuse whatever injustices they did as they opened the peninsula, revolutionized our agriculture and our tourism, built lavish resorts, and brought cities into the spotlight nationally that would have otherwise been ignored. But they did more for Florida than many of our elected officials, who have certainly done worse to both the environment and Florida's first people. But what I hope you take away with you is that these two men, born of another America, forever altered the face of Florida and without them, it wouldn't be the state we know today—and without their healthy, mostly friendly competition, they wouldn't likely have done what they did and created the state we love.

5

The Great Depression

Down, But Never Out

Both Flagler and Plant were fortunate they didn't live to see their empires destroyed and parceled out during the Great Depression. Plant's beloved Tampa Bay Hotel closed during the Depression, and Flagler's Eighth Wonder of the World, destroyed in a hurricane, would never get rebuilt.

The 1930s in America were rough, but in Florida, things were already hard by the time the stock market crashed on Black Tuesday. Black Tuesday, you likely remember from your high school history class, was when Wall Street fell because investors panicked, sold massive amounts of stock, and the banks, which were not federally insured at the time, didn't have enough money for the people who wanted their money *right now*.

Most people think of Black Tuesday as the start of the Great Depression, a herald of hard times ahead for most of America. In Florida, though, the hard times had already arrived. Let's travel back to say, a Florida day in summertime, 1930.

This summer day in 1930 is already difficult because there is no air conditioning. In the mid-nineteenth century, John Gorrie secured a patent for the precursor to air conditioning, a machine that made ice. Willis Havilland Carrier built on Gorrie's ice machine and invented air conditioning in 1902, but until the mid-twentieth century, only places like movie theaters and the homes of the wealthiest Floridians had air conditioning. That meant it would likely be the same temperature inside your home as out, if not hotter, and you relied on windows that opened on a slant—called jalousie windows—and roofs that overhung the building to offer shade from the sun and relief from the rain. Had anyone been foolish enough to build a building like those so popular in Florida today—office buildings with no windows that open and no real overhang to the roof—they would have been mocked mercilessly. Had anyone else been foolish enough to try and live inside of it, in all probability they would have died on a hot summer's day like today. At a minimum, it would have been uncomfortable, which would have been awful. Early Florida residents needed well-ventilated, self-air-conditioned homes quite badly, mostly to escape from the storms and bugs.

Because there was rain, and lots of it. Florida receives almost sixty inches of rain every year, making us the fifth-wettest state in the nation (right after Hawaii, Louisiana, Mississippi, and Alabama). And in 1930, we didn't have as many paved roads as we have today, so that meant the rain could make a whole lot of mud. And puddles. And, of course, we were mostly swamp back then, and swamps are breeding grounds—literally—for mosquitoes. In 1930, the United States Department of Agriculture created a field laboratory in New Smyrna, near Daytona, that dealt with creating ditches in salt marshes. These ditches would help drain land and, in theory, decrease mosquito populations. If you walk outside any contemporary summer night you can see how well this initiative didn't work.

So, simply living in Florida was hard. It was hot, it was wet, and we had more mosquitoes than you can possibly imagine. But that wasn't all. We also had hurricanes, and two in particular—the hurricanes of 1926 and 1928—took huge bites out of Florida's already shaky economy. You see, the prosperity of the 1920s had created a real estate bubble in Florida—where have we heard that before?—that, when it burst (and they always, always burst), left many of the cities destitute. These cities, on the strength of the imminent development, had started building infrastructure such as roads and water systems, while counting on future revenue from taxes and land fees to pay for these improvements. When the bubble burst in 1925, the cities found themselves in serious financial trouble. In 1929, the last remaining Florida industry not already suffering, citrus, was decimated by the Mediterranean fruit fly.

By the time that the stock market fell, well, as Alabama sings in "Song of the South," "we were so broke we couldn't tell."

In 1931, Florida legalized betting at horse and dog tracks as well as on jai alai games. The idea was to collect taxes on the winnings. The problem, of course, was that between the hurricanes and the land bust and the fruit fly, no one had any money to gamble. That same Alabama song continues to tell us, "Mr. Roosevelt is gonna save us all."

Turns out the song was right.

When Franklin D. Roosevelt became president in 1933, he faced a mighty task: fixing a broken country. On August 26, 1935, President Roosevelt signed the Emergency Relief Appropriation Act of 1935, which devoted $4.88 billion to public works projects. Under the auspices of this act, the government created other agencies to help get Americans on their feet and prevent a similar disaster in the future.

Of all the New Deal programs the Civilian Conservation Corps, or the CCC, came to Florida's rescue first, in 1933, before FDR created the WPA. The CCC had some seventy-three camps for young men, both Black and white, in Florida alone. These college-age men received thirty dollars per month for their work, as well as clothes and food; of that, twenty-five dollars went to their mom and dad. They did every kind of manual labor imaginable, from building golf courses to planting flowers and trees. They planted so many trees that people called them the "tree army." You can see statues paying homage to these workers at Florida Caverns State Park, Highlands Hammock State Park, and O'Leno State Park; Highlands Hammock also has a CCC museum.

These were our first lands set aside for state parks, but without national aid it's unlikely we'd have any of them today. The Florida Legislature created the state parks system in 1925, but remember, in 1926, things started going to hell with Florida's economy, and we didn't have any money to build those parks.

Highlands Hammock was one of the first four state parks, and under the WPA, the CCC built five more. This park dates to 1931, two years before the CCC started work. That's because Highlands Hammock opened to the public in 1931 but was still privately owned and didn't have many facilities. It wasn't until 1935 that the state took ownership. Highlands Hammock was built in part by CCC workers and is the first park you should visit to get a sense of how immense the CCC effort was in Florida.

On display at this park's CCC museum are artifacts of CCC work in the nine state parks created by the CCC. Here, Roosevelt's tree army planted trees, built an elevated deck through a swamp, and built roads. The museum pays homage to those young men.

Next to open—on July 4, 1933—was Ravine Gardens, which is exactly what it sounds like: gardens planted along a ravine. All up and down a ravine. And yes, it is fairly unusual to have a ravine in Florida, but this park is in northern Florida, where we start to see some upward elevation not found farther down the peninsula. The park has two ravines, through which Whitewater Branch creek flows. The Civil Works Administration set Palatka's unemployed to planting the walls of the ravine, budgeting more than $160,000 for the project. The effect after eighty-ish years is a rainforest-esque feel at the top that descends into manicured gardens at the base. You get down to the bottom via a downward-sloping brick circle around the perimeter of the ravine.

The park also has a "Garden of States" by the entrance and a nearby sixty-four-foot obelisk dedicated to FDR. They have an azalea festival every year, an homage to the cultivated bushes planted long ago, not the wild native plants that have consumed the ravine with brilliant abandon.

A side note about this park, which has more to do with my own appreciation of food than it does the WPA—not far from here is the oldest diner in Florida, called Angel's. Angel's serves the requisite diner fare of burgers on bulk-purchased buns and crispy fries, but if you're up by Palatka, do yourself a favor and order a Pusalow. I don't know exactly what makes this different from a milkshake, but they're excellent.

Ah, yes, back to the WPA.

If you want to see a real gator—and by real I mean longer than twelve feet—head to Hillsborough River State Park. Although you may not see any at first blush, rest assured, they are indeed there.

This river begins in an area of Florida called the "Green Swamp" and flows through Zephyrhills, Crystal Springs, and downtown Tampa before reaching Tampa Bay. It flows through a bevy of different environments, starting with a swamp and ending in saltwater. The Hillsborough River also provides Tampa Bay Water, a regional water supplier on the southwest coast of Florida, with a portion of its drinking water. The rest of the country has to buy Zephyrhills or Crystal Springs bottled water; in the Tampa Bay area, that water is delivered right to our faucets. That clean, crisp drinking-quality water isn't what motivated the WPA to create a park, though. CCC workers built the park near the rapids. Yes, rapids. In Florida. The Hillsborough River has Class II rapids, which mean they aren't the easiest rapids in the world—that would be Class I—

but they most likely won't kill you, either. One enduring example of the CCC work at Hillsborough River State Park is this suspension bridge. Sixty CCC workers, under the guidance of the National Park Service, built a caretaker's cottage, fire tower, and support buildings. They also built five camping cabins, now gone.

Over by Gainesville, twenty-five craftsmen and several hundred men formed a camp at what is now Mike Roess Gold Head Branch State Park in 1935. The CCC built the nine cabins on Lake Johnson, the ranger station, and the bath house. We visited this park during September, and ours was one of two campers in the park. We never saw anyone enter or leave the other camper, so we may as well have been alone in this vast expanse of lakes and forest. The hiking trails throughout the park are also delightfully narrow—in many places, we walk single file, our trusty hound leashed to avoid crashing off into the woods after any number of unknown animals making alluring sounds—and the path takes you deep into the park, along the edge of the ravine ridge and past the old mill. It's exhilarating in a low-key, Florida way.

Fort Clinch, at the northeastern edge of the state, had military activity starting in 1736, which makes sense, given the site's proximity to the river and the Atlantic at the Florida/Georgia border. Construction on the fort itself began in 1847, and for a short time the fort offered safe harbor for blockade-runners during the Civil War. Blockade-runners, incidentally, is a nicer way of saying "rebel forces"—they were boaters who ensured supplies made it to the Confederacy. Some people call them pirates, some call them freedom fighters—it depends on what else they did other than deliver supplies, the war under discussion, and, quite honestly, the mood of the room when this is discussed.

Whatever one chooses to call them, Confederate supporters used Fort Clinch during the Civil War. Remember, Tallahassee was the only Confederate capital that never fell to the North. The Union did take control of the fort in 1862, however, and used it as a base of operations. Fort Clinch offered great control of South Georgia and North Florida waters. The fort was used again during the Spanish-American War, but right around the turn of the twentieth century, it was left to crumble. The state purchased the land in 1936. When the CCC arrived on-site in the mid-1930s, the fort needed major renovation. CCC workers built the museum, the campsites, and the park's roads. The CCC also worked on restoring the fort, removing 10,000 cubic yards of sand and other debris from the fort, using shovels and wheelbarrows only.

Now, as to what year Fort Clinch became a park? That's interesting, because I couldn't find an answer at the state level. I went through the park's website, the Department of Environmental Protection's management plan for the park, and finally called the state park headquarters, where public relations officers transferred me four times, put me on the phone with a biologist—because that makes sense—who suggested I Google it, and finally give me a date earlier than the park purchase date listed in their own records. I call Fort Clinch, and the nice man on the phone tells me, "I guess about 1937." A friend of mine, upon hearing of my plight—where would I be without Facebook?—went through the archives of the now-defunct *Evening Independent* and found a minuscule article from November 1940, announcing a November 16 ceremony.

I love the story behind O'Leno State Park's name. The park, on the banks of the Santa Fe River, sits on the site of a ghost town originally named Keno. In the mid-1800s, town founders named the town after the game, which is not unlike bingo. When the town applied for a post office in 1876, though, it couldn't get one because the name was associated with gambling. So, the town changed its name to Leno and got a post office. What it didn't get, eighteen years later, was the railroad, and that led to the town's demise. Over the years, people from other towns would come to the site of "Old Leno" for picnics and to swim in the Santa Fe River. In 1935, the Florida Forest Service purchased some land at Old Leno—shortened by then to "O'Leno"—to train forest rangers.

The CCC effort here included workers from High Springs, who built roads, trails, and the bulk of the buildings that remain at the park. O'Leno did indeed train forest rangers before becoming a state park in 1940.

Myakka River State Park opened in 1941. The government purchased seventeen thousand acres of a private estate owned by a woman named Bertha Palmer. This became the core of Myakka River State Park. Of the things built by the CCC, the visitor center, two picnic pavilions, and several of the cabbage palm log cabins used for camping remain, as do the roads. As the South remained deep in the clutches of Jim Crow, Black CCC workers lived in segregated facilities, but they had access to night classes. As historian David Nelson points out, the CCC emphasized educational opportunities even more than work or infrastructure, and the Myakka camp ledgers show that every Black man there enrolled in classes offered by the Corps.

Near the Florida/Georgia/Alabama border, workers would showcase Florida's dry air caves at Florida Caverns State Park. Until 1942, CCC workers worked on and in this park, stopping only when the federal government cut funding. The CCC built the tour caves and a nine-hole golf course as well as a fish hatchery, visitor center, and gift shop. The golf course and fish hatchery are closed, although you can still glimpse the ruins of both. You can take a tour of the dry air caves, something not nearly as common as fish and golf are in Florida. The government only cut funding because at that point most of the country's money—and a great deal of our country's young men—were fighting the Axis Alliance in World War II.

But before funding was cut, the park received a nice chunk of change: the golf course alone received fifty thousand federal dollars and almost as many local ones.

West of Tallahassee, Torreya State Park operated on and off until 1940, and opened fully in 1942. Here grow the last remaining torreya trees in America, so-named for an 1800s botanist, John Torrey. The torreya grows almost exclusively inside the park. Fewer than two hundred of these miniaturized Christmas trees remain, although the tree has distant relatives in Japan and California. This cheerful wisp of greenery—if a tree can be adorable, the torreya is—suffered mightily when Hurricane Michael toppled the canopy of trees the torreya needs to survive, and the once-abundant tree may be in its final hours.

You've heard of torreya trees, but likely not by that name. The torreya tree's alternate name is gopherwood. In case you aren't up on your Old Testament, that's the tree Noah used to build the ark. Of course, the epic flood happened nowhere near the Apalachicola River, although Florida gets its share of rain.

The Apalachicola River lies about 150 feet down from the park, which abuts a ravine far above it, with the Gregory House perched at the top of the ravine. CCC workers dismantled this plantation house and moved it across the river piece by piece, with thoughts of using it as a hotel. There, CCC workers restored it, although the 1849 home never functioned as a hotel. The home serves as one of the few remaining examples of pre–Civil War architecture in Florida.

The CCC started work here in 1935 and continued work at the park until the WPA disbanded the CCC in 1942. The park opened a little bit in 1940—this was another instance where I had to call the park manager, who dug through some old files and helped puzzle through the actual opening date. He told me the public could access parts of the park in 1940 but not all of it until 1942. We speculate that perhaps the whole "dismantling a house, moving it across the river, and reassembling it" was part of the motivation to keep people out of the park—and out of harm's way—for a time. The CCC workers were great, but if anyone's ever seen a group of nineteen-year-old boys working on something en masse, you know that safety isn't always foremost in their mind. I had a park ranger once describe young men as "YIMS"—young, immortal males.

Of the money FDR earmarked for WPA efforts, $27 million went to what would become known as Federal One. Federal One consisted of writing, art, and theater—the Federal Art Project, the Federal Theatre Project, and the Federal Writers' Project. It also included the Federal Music Project.

One of Federal One's most enduring works is the American Guide series. In each state, the Federal Writers' Project paid writers who had no jobs and no prospects (which I like to remind people is essentially all writers) to create driving tours of that state.

The brilliance of these WPA tours became apparent after Eisenhower built the interstates that encouraged drivers to bypass small town after small town in favor of making good time. Today, the absence of the American Guide series is keenly felt, especially in Florida, where most guidebooks barely scratch the state's surface. These roads lay forgotten by all but the local residents, a few commuters, and dedicated road-trippers actively seeking such roads.

In 1937, the Florida Writers' Project sent writers—mostly anonymous writers, but also Zora Neale Hurston and a still-wet-behind-the-ears Stetson Kennedy—into the depths of Florida to reveal its splendor to the world. What they found wasn't always splendid; they encountered mosquitoes, slave-like working conditions, racism, and poverty. But these writers did reveal to the world Florida's beauty in all its forms. They wrote about thick green forests, white sand beaches, and waters teeming with seafood. In 1939, the FWP and the State of Florida jointly published the work of these writers as *A Guide to the Southernmost State.*

Zora's value to the WPA was as a folklorist, trained as an anthropologist and writer and able to do exactly what Federal One needed people to do. While "folklorist" is not something you see advertised in the classifieds, it is a real job. A folklorist is someone who collects culture. They study traditions of a group and document how they live.

Of course, this was 1930s Florida, so the bulk of her work involved infiltrating Black communities and telling the stories she found. She did such a brilliant job, though, that the final guide—and the WPA produced a separate "Negro" book—is peppered with her forays into Black communities and labor camps. The Federal Writers' Project sent her to Black areas: Ocoee, Eatonville, Pahokee, and Goldsboro.

During her second and final year working on the Federal Writers' Project, 1939, Hurston traveled to Cross City in Dixie County to find people who would talk to her. She wanted to record interviews and songs and take in oral histories.

She found turpentine.

She recorded people giving interviews, singing songs, and telling their life histories. She didn't want to talk to well-known people; she wanted to talk to the people no one looked at twice. She wanted to talk to the Black men working in turpentine camps. She wrote an essay called, appropriately, "Turpentine," which took the reader on a journey with her through Florida's pine forests.

Lest you think the WPA efforts in Florida consisted of writing books and hanging out in the prettiest parts of the state, let's move on to some other projects the WPA undertook to salvage the Sunshine State.

WPA workers did less glamorous work, work of amazing importance often forgotten in the discussion of art deco buildings and creating a state park system. Because of the WPA, Pensacola has storm sewers. The Civil Works Administration and other WPA agencies made improvements to the City of Neptune Beach's water systems and streets, and also to its bulkheads, which would keep the city from flooding. The WPA funded a seawall on Lake Apopka in Winter Garden. They built an entire sewer system in Key West, the very existence of which has probably done more to preserve the island's tourist industry than any one other thing. Septic systems, you see, don't work so well when your backyard is only a couple feet of limestone before you hit saltwater. A boat used to carry the sewage from Key West outhouses and dump it in the ocean. The sewage would be placed into fifty-five-gallon drums for dumping.

No treatment, no nothing—just dump it overboard and hope it doesn't find its way back to the island.

WPA projects are among some of the most shining examples of how Florida took its struggles and did more than survive. For instance, the destroyed Over-the-Sea Railroad line in the Florida Keys was converted to the Overseas Highway. Seventy miles off the coast of Key West sits Fort Jefferson, where CCC workers renovated the crumbling fort's structure and also performed historic restoration. Fort Jefferson isn't simply a national park—it was a crucial part of our maritime defense. The WPA assumed control of an abandoned work camp in Ocala, Camp Roosevelt, and, in conjunction with the University of Florida, converted it into an adult education center. They trained people for better jobs, for jobs they could take after the WPA efforts ended and there were no more sewers or roads to build.

The WPA effort didn't last a full decade. In 1942 the United States disbanded the CCC. War had provided its own economic stimulus, and for the next several years, the US turned its focus to that, not infrastructure. It would be another decade before work would resume on Florida's state parks, but President Roosevelt's temporary relief programs forever altered Florida. Between 1935 and 1943, the official dates the WPA and its subsidiaries existed, the federal government provided 8 million jobs—in and out of Florida. CCC workers built ninety-nine buildings in the nine Florida state parks they created. In total, the WPA spent $13.4 billion. Adjusted for inflation, that's $233.4 billion, or roughly $29.2 billion a year. That may sound like a lot—because it is—but the benefits to Florida (and, of course, to all the states) and the people who, years later, call the Sunshine State home—are eternal.

The WPA is their legacy, but it is our providence.

6

~~~~~~

Eatonville

Zora, Community, and Hope

Every so many weeks I find myself camping in a different Florida state park. As I'm sure I've written—either in this tome or on my blog or newsletter or simply called out to the ether—Florida has the best state parks.

At least one of them was built wholly by Black men: Myakka River State Park. And, while Black men worked in other CCC camps, every time I visit a CCC park lately, it seems I'm hit in the face with more evidence of Black men doing more to build Florida than we've ever previously recognized.

But what about Black women?

As I write this, the Zora Neale Hurston quote from *Their Eyes Were Watching God* rings in my head. I won't quote it directly because she used words I can and will not, but it essentially reminds everyone that the Black woman is "de mule uh de world so far as Ah can see."

I don't change the language because, for Zora, quoting Black people as Black people spoke was a hill upon which she would die. Black people spoke different, and as much as her Harlem friends such as Langston Hughes would entreat her to make them "speak white," she would not. This falling-out cost her dearly, in terms of her career, and Zora herself died a pauper, buried in a forgotten and unmarked grave in Fort Pierce, Florida, more than one hundred miles from her hometown, in January 1960. Almost four decades later she would, one final time, become the voice of her people and help protect her hometown of Eatonville.

Visit Eatonville today and you won't find much to amuse you. There's no Disney-esque attraction; no flourishing historical center at which you can buy books and guide maps to Zora's childhood home. Why, it's almost as if Eatonville doesn't need the white tourist at all for it to exist.

And that, of course, is at the key of Eatonville's survival. Eatonville is not a *tourist* town; it's a *home*town. And, while it's a town not without its challenges, it's one that persists in whole mostly because of Zora.

Even if she never knew it would come to that at all.

Let's go back to Zora's birth, which, despite her assertion otherwise, didn't happen in Eatonville, but in Notasulga, Alabama. She'd deny that through her life, saying she'd been born in Eatonville, Florida, and though we historians believe now that's not the case, not a single one of us can blame her, because Eatonville has a case for the spectacular.

"I was born in a Negro town," Hurston wrote in *Dust Tracks on the Road*. "I do not mean by that the Black back-side of an average town. Eatonville, Florida, is, and was at the time of my birth, a pure Negro town—charter, mayor, council, town marshal and all."

While there's much to be—and much that has been—written about that town's simple existence, there's a great triumph for that town that speaks to the human desire—Black, white, or anyone—to preserve a way of life.

The town, though named for a neighboring white mayor, Josiah Eaton, of Maitland, had its own identity. In 1887, twenty-seven Black men organized the town, making it the first all-Black town (including its leadership) in the US.

That this would happen in Florida—in the South, as this area of Florida counts as the Deep, not New, South—seems discordant.

Nearby, dark, evil things happened to Black people: Thirteen miles away, in Ocoee, the Ku Klux Klan murdered Black citizens legally attempting to vote on November 1, 1920. Forty miles away, in 1949, police arrested four Black men, all four wrongfully accused of raping a white woman. White men killed one of the Groveland Four before the case went to trial; Lake County sheriff Willis McCall killed another of the four young men, claiming that, despite being handcuffed, the young man tried to escape. The other two men spent serious prison time. (In 2019, in his first days in office, Florida governor Ron DeSantis pardoned the foursome, calling their convictions "a miscarriage of justice"; in 2021, Lake County judge Heidi Davis took it a step further and exonerated the men.) Fifty miles away, assassins set a bomb under the bed of

NAACP activists Harry and Harriette Moore. They'd gone to bed after celebrating their twenty-fifth wedding anniversary on Christmas night, 1951. Harry died before the ambulance could get him to a doctor; Harriette died nine days later, earning the couple the horrific, dubious honor of being the first people killed in the civil rights movement.

Throughout the Jim Crow South and repeated mass killings of Black men, women, and children that followed the end of the Civil War, Eatonville offered hope to Black southerners; it afforded not only independence but also a place where Black people could live with less fear. While racial injustices swirled around Eatonville, the small town soldiered on, led skillfully by a Black mayor and Black town council at a time where, in other parts of the South, Black people lived in fear of false accusations and real lynchings.

Over time, though, the subtle fingers of racism have attempted to form a fist that would smash the town, if given the chance, and it's fallen to the residents who call this piece of paradise home to defend their land against what state and county leaders call "progress."

Somewhere between 1964 and 1966, I-4 slapped its ridiculously large (though time would show, not large enough to accommodate all the tourists) footsteps through the town, bisecting—but not allowing an exit at—Eatonville.

This, says NYU law professor and president of the ACLU Deborah Archer, happened across the country, often by design, offering scared white people quiet, yet targeted and effective, backlash against Black people benefiting at last from courts ruling in favor of civil rights–minded legislation.

To get to Eatonville today, drivers have to exit I-4—driving on which offers adventure enough, and not in the fun, "riding the teacups at Disney" sense of the word, but in the "Dante's ninth circle of hell" sense—and exercise a series of driving maneuvers and acrobatics for which the average SUV is not designed.

With no exit comes none of the detritus of the Eisenhower interstate system: Eatonville has no corporate gas stations with litter accumulating at its corners, no blight of signs advertising the calorie-rich, nutrient-poor fast-food chains whose salaries cannot sustain an adult with bills to pay, no cigarette butts accumulating at stoplights as interstate drivers pull off to get gas or greasy fried food. But it also has none of the benefits: without the tax revenue from these types of businesses, the onus of survival falls squarely on the shoulders of the roughly 2,300 people who call Eatonville home. To put it another way, the town must subsist on the property taxes of not even one thousand homes.

When Orange County wanted to widen Kennedy Boulevard—the town's main road would have become a traffic sewer—and build a medical waste incinerator, and then a bevy of adult entertainment venues—the people of the town had enough. And they found a way to stop it.

Zora.

In 1987, the Association to Preserve the Eatonville Community (PEC) came into existence. During its first years it served as an advocacy group, working to halt the widening of the town's main street while also promoting historic preservation.

In 1989, PEC hosted the inaugural Zora Neale Hurston Festival of Arts and Humanities. Over the years this annual event has drawn thousands of attendees to hear Maya Angelou, Alice Walker, and other notable Americans speak.

Today known as *Zora!*, the festival celebrates spirituality through an Afrotourism lens. Organizers started meeting to stop the road, which they called "community busting" (and they were not wrong), and today continue to work toward preserving Eatonville's unusual and spectacular community and character.

One final note about Eatonville and Zora: While the town itself remains, as I said, a hometown, not a tourist town, if you want to get a sense of the place, find a copy of *Their Eyes Were Watching God*. In that work, Hurston showcased the heartbreak of and injustices committed against Black families at the mercy of not only the white farmers, but the brute force of Florida's harshest weather: the hurricane that dealt the final blow to the state's already-shaky late-1920s economy.

7

Hurricanes

Saffir, Simpson, and Florida's Paul Revere

If Florida needed the WPA before of the rest of America, you can credit hurricanes. Specifically, the hurricanes of 1926 and 1928. And while those may be two of Florida's most significant hurricanes—the others including, at press time, the Labor Day Hurricane of 1935, Hurricane Andrew in 1992, Hurricane Michael in 2018, and Hurricane Ian in 2022—every hurricane presents a little differently in Florida, and our history with these great storms is nothing short of spectacular.

Take Hurricane Irma. In 2017, Hurricane Irma was bearing down on Florida. I'd just finished the draft of this chapter, and I was apoplectic looking at the probable storm tracks. All I could think was, "history is repeating and we haven't learned a damn thing."

In 2011, *Backroads of Paradise*, my first book, was still coming together. I worked during the day and wrote into the night. My not-yet husband would go to bed at a decent hour, and I would stay up, writing. The night I finished the chapter on SR 80 and the Hurricane of 1928, I was in tears. Not a lone trickle down a cheek, either; I was hard-core sobbing. My beloved stumbled out of the bedroom at 3:00 a.m. and asked me, "what's wrong?"

"All those people," I gulped through not-very-pretty tears. "They died!"

"What? Where?" he asked, assuming—as most people would—that some new tragedy had befallen America while he slept. "When?"

"In Okeechobee. The hurricane." When he looked more confused, I choked out, "In 1928."

He sighed.

"Close the laptop and come to bed, OK?"

In 2017, I watched the track for Irma and then fervently consulted my notes. They were, for a time, the same. And the levee was ready to break again. Fortunately, the track changed. Irma swerved. The land—and, more importantly, the lives south of Lake Okeechobee—were spared.

But that's how hurricane season goes down here; we're a swinging-trapeze mess of "whoo-hoo, gonna rain a bit, let's enjoy that day off, Hurricane Party!" and "OH MY GOD WE ARE ALL GOING TO DIE."

People like to say Florida doesn't have seasons, and there's a joke that goes "sure we do—hurricane season, snowbird season . . . ," and while that's underselling the natural beauty and environmental changes of the state, there's no denying we have a hurricane season.

Officially, hurricane season starts on June 1 and lasts through November 30—half of the year. Floridians know, however, that the threats don't get real until August. The vast majority of hurricanes that come within two hundred nautical miles of either Pensacola or Miami have historically done so between August and October, although on November 12, 2020, Hurricane Eta brushed close enough to the Tampa Bay area that it pushed storm surge high enough that the Christmas tree in downtown Gulfport was several feet underwater, which dovetailed nicely with the way the rest of 2020 was breaking. So when the counties launch their hurricane awareness parties (we can call them hurricane conferences, but I've witnessed the air of gleeful anticipation) in May, and we start having sales tax holidays for hurricane supplies, well, honestly, we're all just so damn happy to have those regular thundershowers to break up the heat that we're delighted it's storm season again. After all, August and the two months after it all feel far away.

But why those three months? What about those months makes the magic, and hey, while we're asking questions, why does a storm that brings about loss of life and property qualify for making Florida spectacular, anyway?

As you'll see, it's not the storms themselves but how Florida handles them—and how that experience helps the rest of the country adapt as climate change brings more storms to more places—that adds to the Florida spectacular.

First, the basics—how does a hurricane form? According to the National Oceanic and Atmospheric Administration (NOAA), a hurricane, or a tropical cyclone, "is a rotating low-pressure weather system that has organized thunderstorms but no fronts (a boundary separating two air masses of different densities)." But unless you're a weather geek or a general aviation pilot, that sounds like gibberish. Let's break it down.

A "weather system" is either stable or unstable. And it has a lot to do with what meteorologists call isobars. Isobars are a visual mapmaking referent to show how much pressure the atmosphere is applying to the earth, rendered as lines connecting weather systems that have the same amount of pressure. Think of that pressure as the weight of the air, getting pulled to earth by earth's gravity. We measure this pressure with a barometer, and we measure it in millibars.

There are two types of pressure systems—high and low—and pressure is tied to temperature. We see more high-pressure systems when it's colder. Think of cold air as heavier than warm air, which makes it easier for the earth's gravity to pull the cold air to the surface of the earth, which creates a high-pressure system. A high-pressure weather system is stable, because in these conditions it's harder for clouds to form. You can feel a light wind perhaps, but there won't be many clouds in the sky. This is also why we tend to have drier winters than summers—because it's colder. Meteorologists consider a barometer reading of 1013.25 millibars as high pressure.

We see more low-pressure systems when it's warmer, because warm air isn't as heavy, so to speak, as cold air, and the earth's gravitational pull can't pull the air down to the surface as easily—there's lower pressure. A low-pressure system is unstable, because it's easier for clouds to form and accumulate. This is why we have such wet summers: it's warmer with more air mixing than in the winter. Meteorologists consider a barometer reading of 984 millibars as low pressure.

In a low-pressure system in the Northern Hemisphere, the air currents around the system move toward the center of the system in a counterclockwise direction. Now we have a low-pressure rotating weather system, and if it doesn't run into a high-pressure system and become a "front," we'll get a hurricane.

So, what's the perfect recipe for a hurricane?

To make a hurricane, you need to have warm air in the Atlantic basin, which includes the Gulf of Mexico, the Atlantic Ocean, the Caribbean, and, believe it or not, the eastern North Pacific Ocean and, rarely, the central North Pacific. That's because the air that rises over water will be warm and moisture-filled, and as that air that flows toward the center collects and rises, it cools, and the moisture in it forms clouds.

The next thing that needs to happen is that those isobars have to be pretty closely grouped, or, more simply, there must be many low-pressure systems close together. When there's warm, moist air and tightly spaced isobars, the system will start to feed off the surrounding air, sucking it in and pushing that toward the center, too. As it grows, it spins faster. This is when we start to see a clearly defined "eye" of the storm. The eye of the storm is the area of lowest pressure. The eye of the storm is clear and calm.

If the sustained winds—not the gusts—around the eye aren't at least 39 mph, we call this a tropical depression. One the maximum sustained winds are 40 mph, we call it a tropical storm. And, of course, once those winds reach 74 mph, they become tropical cyclones, which we also call hurricanes if they form in the Atlantic basin or in the eastern Pacific Ocean. Everywhere else they're tropical cyclones, and, in some areas, we call them typhoons. That's because of Caribbean mythology.

Kulucan was the Mayan spirit of the storm, also called the one-legged god. In many images of him, you can see the spinning clouds around his leg, and in at least one such image, the artist identifies Kulucan as "Hurukan." Hurukan is really Huraca'n, which is Taíno. Taíno are the indigenous peoples in the Caribbean, and to them, Huruca'n was the spirit of an angry woman goddess who rode the winds, named Guabancex (*GWA-bah-sah*). Guabancex had two male companions, twin gods named Guatauba (*gwa-ta-ooh-BA*), the god of thunder, and Coatrisque (*ko-ah-tris-keh*), the god of wind. As a threesome, they combined to form the wind, thunder, and flood spirits of the Huruca'n.

When the Spanish first started exploring the Caribbean and La Florida, one conquistador wrote that the Taíno said, "when Guabancex becomes angry, she makes the winds and waters move and casts houses to the ground and uproots the trees."

An image from Taíno pottery, which well predates any satellite imagery of hurricanes, shows Guabancex, arms rotating—in the same directions as a hurricane's winds do.

Florida recorded its first major hurricane on August 23, 1851, and it was the second recorded hurricane to come to the US—the first was a Category 1 that headed for Texas on June 25 of that same year. This is not to say weather started getting crazy in 1851; this is when the record-keeping started. NOAA refers to it as the Great Middle Florida Hurricane, because geographic identifiers were the initial manner of identifying storms; of course, it ultimately became clear we would have many hurricanes named, say, the Great South Florida Hurricane, so that had to change. The Great Middle Florida Hurricane had a central pressure of 960 millibars and maximum recorded winds of 100 mph. This made it a Category 3 on the Saffir Simpson scale.

The Saffir-Simpson scale sounds fancy, but down here we live by it for a few months every year, making it not so much fancy as it is familiar—although most of us probably couldn't tell you who Saffir and Simpson were. Here's where Florida starts to get spectacular because of our hurricanes.

Robert Simpson took over as director of the National Hurricane Center (NHC) in 1967 and immediately realized that no matter what a great job the NHC did, unless it could find an easily digestible way of explaining hurricanes—and how dangerous they could be—to the masses, all the work the NHC did wouldn't be of much use. Four years later, in 1971, he and Herbert Saffir, a civil engineer, developed the scale we use today. It initially included storm surge and pressure readings, but in 2009 the NHC eliminated everything but wind. And it's important to realize that a Category 1 that hits, say, Miami, will result in higher cumulative damage levels than a Category 5 would in a completely rural area (although since hurricanes weaken over land, this isn't likely).

While it's a wind scale, and while it you can still use the scale as a guesstimate for other things, it's important to remember that all the categories mean is how strong the maximum winds are. They're not an indication of gusts that may go higher or storm surge, although they do offer some guidelines for that—and we have historical data to tell us how high a storm surge does relate to wind speed.

Let's start with the worst hurricanes first, so by the time you finish this chapter, you feel better, not worse, about hurricanes. Also, this is where everyone's mind goes when we hear the word "hurricane"—the Category 5. A Cat 5 means the winds are at least 157 mph. That's pretty bad. According to NOAA, "Catastrophic damage will occur: A high percentage of framed homes will be destroyed, with total roof failure and wall collapse. Fallen trees and power poles will isolate residential areas. Power outages will last for weeks to possibly months. Most of the area will be uninhabitable for weeks or months."

We first recorded Cat 5 in 1924, but the first Cat 5 in Florida was the hurricane of 1928. Of course, by the time it hit Florida, it was "only" a Cat 4—and we'll get to those later.

The first Cat 5 to have a Cat 5 impact on Florida? That was the Labor Day Hurricane of 1935. And this story—well, it's heartbreaking.

This happened well before the days of radar and Doppler and hurricane reconnaissance planes. So the earliest indication we have of this hurricane forming was August 29, 1935—east and north of Turks Island. Four days later, the hurricane made landfall in the Florida Keys, when the eye was reported at about ten miles long—and the storm moved at only 10 mph, which is never good, because the slower the storm, the more air it can suck in and the bigger it can grow. The maximum sustained winds when it came ashore were 185 miles per hour—and remember, those are sustained winds; winds gusted upward of 200 MPH.

Keep in mind, our early warning system in the 1930s was "warning blocks" that planes that would drop on low-lying areas, like the coast, warning of the impending storm and asking folks to warn their neighbors. Not exactly effective.

A storm surge between four-and-a-half feet and six feet completely covered the low-lying chain of islands, and the storm destroyed every structure on Matecumbe Key, which is part of Islamorada.

We had World War I veterans working in the Florida Keys as part of the WPA. They worked in the Upper Keys—think Key Largo and Islamorada—and at 2:00 p.m. on Labor Day, 1935, Fred Ghent, who was the assistant administrator of the Federal Emergency Relief Administration, ordered a train to evacuate the Upper Keys veterans. Because of complications of the storm, it wouldn't arrive until roughly 8:20 that night. When it did, the storm swept the train off its tracks. Miraculously, none of the veterans on that train died. However, three veterans' work camps were completely destroyed, and an estimated 250 veterans died. Many of them have unmarked graves in the Keys; others were sent to Woodlawn Cemetery in Miami for a mass burial. Both of these things, by the way, violate federal law—veterans are entitled to an individual grave and headstone.

In 2015 I met a survivor in Islamorada who was a child when the hurricane hit. Eighty years after the storm, his memories were still vivid and heartbreaking. Some of his family died, but he said he can only assume this because their bodies were never found. Other survivors told stories of how the force of the wind was so strong that the sand ripped off people's clothes.

The hurricane did all its damage in Florida, but the worst damage was in the Florida Keys, where it cut a sixty-four-mile swath of total devastation, stretching from Key Largo to Marathon. Almost five hundred people died. According to the 1935 census, only one thousand people lived in the Keys outside of Key West. The number grew after the storm and over the years because, at first rescue workers, who had arrived with food and water and supplies but found no survivors, kept finding dead bodies. Over the years, people would find skeletons of storm victims. Meteorologists recorded the lowest pressure ever for a storm—892 millibars—and this is, by all accounts, the strongest storm to ever make landfall in the US. The thinking after the storm was that errors from the Weather Bureau contributed to the death toll because it mis-forecast the storm, predicting it would head through the Florida Straits and turn north. Initially, the storm was smaller, too—and it grew over the course of the weekend but moved more slowly than expected, so by the time it turned and it was clear it would make landfall, there was little anyone could do. Remember, the only way back to the mainland was by boat or train, and since it was a single track, only one train could run at a time. It was 5:00 p.m. before a train could leave Homestead and get to the Keys. It backed down the track, but only covered forty-five miles before the storm overtook it and tossed it off the track. There was no way for anyone to get out.

One account tells of a woman blown forty miles over the sea from Islamorada to Cape Sable. While she apparently lived long enough to crawl up the shoreline, when the Coast Guard found her she was dead, still holding the body of her dead son.

After the storm, FDR ordered the VA to lead an investigation, assisted by the Federal Emergency Relief Administration, into whether or not the government was to blame for the veterans' deaths. FERA, independent of the VA, released its report to the media on September 8, saying the storm was an act of God and therefore the government wasn't to blame. The VA, however, continued its investigation, and on October 30 it released a report saying it did find negligence. Neither agency would compromise, and the joint report never came to pass.

Today you can find a limestone monument to the victims of the storm in Islamorada, just south of the Keys History & Discovery Center.

This was the strongest hurricane to touch the mainland. In 1992, we had another hurricane strike the mainland—Andrew, in Miami and Homestead. I traveled through Miami and Homestead the month after the storm, and all I remember is devastation—some older buildings on Krome Avenue still had their facades, but the homes had no roofs and many walls were gone. You would see things in odd places—bikes wrapped around poles, random bits of furniture in lakes. There were no street signs, or any signs at all, to speak of. People were without power for weeks; ice was sold at a premium.

Much of the destruction, reports later found, came from construction not built to code—mobile homes, for example, are supposed to have tie-down straps, and investigators found many with none ever installed. This blame fell with Miami-Dade's building department.

A Category 4 has winds up to 155 mph. The most haunting tale of a Cat 4 happened before our first Cat 5, in 1928. That hurricane, which Elliot Kleinberg wrote about extensively in *Black Cloud*, devastated South Florida—especially the farmers south of Lake Okeechobee, where in hindsight they never should have lived to begin with. Here's the problem with putting houses down in this part of Florida: the land is low and wet, and no matter what humans try to do to make it higher and drier, the fix sticks only in the short term. The hurricane of 1928 proved this. In the early 1920s, as Florida swelled with people intent on bending paradise to their will, the land south of Lake Okeechobee caught the eye of farmers. Seems millennia of optimal conditions (limestone, high rainfall levels, land that doesn't slope that much, plant life aplenty on that land growing, dying and decaying) created rich black muck that would grow, well, almost anything. And it was a lot of muck, "largest single body of organic soils in the world"—scientists estimated the muck, at one point, was seventeen feet deep directly south of Okeechobee.

"At the beginning of the twentieth century, water simply flowed unimpeded from the lake's south shore in a sheet, into the Everglades. . . . For the early settlers and farmers, that simply would not do. So between 1923 and 1925, the state built a 47-mile-long dike of earth. It was about five feet high. Twice in the next three years, it would be shown as useless as a dam made of tissue paper.

"In the early 1920s, commissioners of the Everglades Drainage District, founded in 1913, decided to build a more permanent dike around Lake Okeechobee. The plan was for work to start on the dike in 1927. It would be 110 to 130 feet wide at the base and 20 feet wide at the crest and stand 27 feet above sea level. They concluded that such a levee would resist hurricane-driven surge from the lake. But the legislature didn't get around to approving the money for it."[1]

What's so senseless about the deaths of 1928 was that the same thing happened in 1926, but on a much smaller scale. When the 1926 hurricane, called the Miami Hurricane, hit Florida on September 18, 1926, a low dirt dike burst at Moore Haven, a town of 1,200. Estimates say the water rose seventeen feet, destroying the under-construction Glades County Courthouse. Officials buried the unidentifiable bodies in a mass county grave.

In the case of the 1926 hurricane, forecasters didn't notify people in time. Initially, although ships had notified authorities about a hurricane offshore, the US Weather Bureau said the storm wouldn't hit South Florida. They were wrong. People received the hurricane warning right before the hurricane made landfall.[2]

Almost four hundred people died—officially. However, given the historic lack of consideration given to poor Black laborers in the aftermath of a hurricane, many historians believe this number might be inaccurate.

One of the reasons people died was a result of the 1920s land boom in Florida, which had made Miami the fastest-growing city in the United States. Northerners, unfamiliar with hurricanes, didn't realize the eye of the storm wasn't the *end* of the storm, so they left wherever they had sheltered during the first part of the storm. When the eye passed and the back side of the hurricane hit, they fell victim to a ten-foot storm surge and debris flying through the air at up to 155 mph.

Damage from the storm totaled $105 million—and that's in 1926 dollars. Calculated for inflation, that amount would be $1.56 billion in 2021 dollars. However, given the size of Miami today, scientists and economists agree that a similar storm would cause $157 billion in 2005 dollars. This sent Miami—and most of Florida—into the Great Depression three years ahead of the rest of the country.

The Miami Hurricane didn't only damage South Florida, however—it continued on to Pensacola, where it struck Florida again and raged for twenty hours on September 20, destroying essentially every wharf, building, and boat in the city. After that, it finally made landfall a third time in Mobile, Alabama.

When we talk about the winds of the Miami Hurricane, it's impossible to know the exact speed, because those winds destroyed the equipment used to measure wind. Despite the seventeen-foot storm surge in Moore Haven when one part of the mud dike burst in the 1926 hurricane, that promised work on the levee in 1927 work never started. As you can imagine, by September 1928, the dikes hadn't gotten better with age, but area farms still flourished in that productive black muck. Heavy late-summer rains and storms dumped more water in the lake. When a hurricane made landfall on September 16, water dammed in Okeechobee had nowhere to go.

The water crashed though the dike, a tidal wave of watery destruction, upending houses and flipping cars, drowning children and adults with no sense of honor. The stench of death lingered for weeks, haunting survivors—left to bury the dead—until they, too, were about to meet death.

In 2018, Hurricane Michael hit Florida as a Category 5, and it wrought, sadly, predictable devastation to the coastal Panhandle. As it moved inland, though, something less predictable happened: Michael weakened—but not enough. It swept through inland parks; at Torreya State Park, it leveled the canopy, putting the park's critically endangered namesake tree whispers from extinction.

Wildlife biologists did not have a plan for hurricane devastation for the torreya; the species survival plan addressed the possibility of fire, not hurricane-force winds.

Slightly west of Torreya State Park, downed trees trapped the Florida Caverns State Park manager in his home on park property for days. While Hurricane Michael certainly caused devastation for humans along the coast—officials say almost sixty people died in the US as a result of Michael—the damage inland, both to the natural environment and homes previously too far inland to worry about wind deductibles, presented new challenges for those who live and work and love Florida.

A Category 4 or 5 is nothing to play with.

From there, it's not as bad. Cat 3? Heck, why even get out of bed? In 1960, Hurricane Donna was another Category 4 storm that weakened to a Cat 3 by the time it hit Florida, with "only" 120 mph winds and "only" 13 fatalities—six people drowned, four people had heart attacks, two died in car crashes, and two were electrocuted. Almost 1,200 others were injured, but the fatalities were way down. Why?

Well, officials had made some advances in how they monitored and tracked hurricanes. Starting in the late nineteenth century, it became clear we needed a better way to track hurricanes. This is also, you'll note, when people started moving to Florida in earnest.

After a fairly active 1934 hurricane season and one huge misstep from a DC map plotter at the National Weather Service, things changed. According to Gordon Dunn, who at one time was the head of the Weather Bureau Office Miami, "a tropical storm formed in late August 1934 in the central Gulf of Mexico and on Sunday forenoon the Washington-based forecaster issued a hurricane warning for the Upper Texas coast. Since there would be no additional observations until 7 p.m., the forecaster, as usual, went home, planning to return in the evening to issue the regular and hurricane forecasts. In Galveston, which had continued to be an area sensitive (to hurricane threats) since the 1900 disaster, the populace scanned the sky for indications of the forecast hurricane. It was moving more slowly than the morning advisory indicated and weather conditions remained serene. Finally, by mid afternoon, the anxious Chamber of Commerce wired the Washington Weather Bureau for the latest information. The map plotter on duty honestly, but indiscreetly, wired back: 'Forecaster on golf course—unable to contact.' In Galveston the weather remained quiet, but temperatures in the Chamber of Commerce rose rapidly."

Now, odds are you can tell me what George Washington, Abraham Lincoln, Franklin Roosevelt, and Barack Obama did for our country, but can anyone name one thing William McKinley did? Well, in 1898, President William McKinley ordered the Weather Bureau to set up a weather center devoted to hurricanes. The Weather Bureau Office moved from Jupiter to Miami in 1900. Richard Gray was the first what they called "Official in Charge" at the Miami Hurricane Center. The earliest warning systems, as mentioned, were lacking, as was the equipment for detecting hurricanes. In the case of the 1926 hurricane, for example, the indications of a hurricane were that the barometer was dropping and the winds were increasing. This happened as the hurricane was bearing down on Miami, and if you read the archived copy of the 1926 reports of the hurricane, there are reports of Gray, in an effort to warn people, running through the streets of Miami, screaming as loud as he could that a hurricane was coming, sort of a Paul Revere for Florida. After the hurricane of 1935, Congress approved $128,000 to improve hurricane tracking. In 1966, the Miami office officially became the National Hurricane Center, and one year later Dr. Robert H. Simpson took over—yes, of the Saffir-Simpson wind scale. Since 1966, the NHC has had the primary responsibility for forecasting hurricanes anywhere in the Atlantic basin.

Now, before we leave Category 3 hurricanes—which is where we started discussing the history of the NHC—I want to mention that the first Category 3 with a name was Hurricane Easy, the fifth storm of the 1950 season. The NHC first started naming storms in 1950, using the Joint Army/Navy Phonetic Alphabet, which meant the first five hurricanes were named, in order, Abe, Baker, Charlie, Dog and Easy. That same season also included Tropical Storm How, Hurricane Item, Hurricane Jig, and Hurricane Love. We've, uh, gotten better at naming storms. Easy, by the way, made landfall at Cedar Key, went offshore, made a nice little loop, and made landfall again at Hernando Beach. The names are used again every six years, except when a storm has been especially brutal and the name gets "retired."

I'm going to combine the last two categories because their stories, of course, are not as dramatic. Category 2 storms we've seen relatively recently are 2004's Hurricane Frances and 2016's Hurricane Matthew. Interesting to note is that for all the horrors Katrina caused in New Orleans, it was a Category 1 in Florida, which puts it on the same level as Hermine, Nate, and Otto—not exactly some of Florida's biggest-named storms.

Look, if you're in the path of a Category 3, 2, or 1—I'm not saying don't take it seriously. But years ago, I worked at a local radio station, and we had a standing order from some advertisers that as soon as there was a named storm, we were to run certain ads. Hurricanes are awful for coastal dwellers, but they're big money for Home Depot, The Weather Channel, and plywood companies. So it does seem as though the hype can get overblown. And I don't watch the news—I read the reports and forecasts at hurricanes.gov, which is where every meteorologist in the country gets their information too—the rest is conjecture and, often, offered to the viewers in a way to get them to keep tuning in.

When you read the advisories from the NHC, you can tell certain forecasters have certain personalities. My favorite is Forecaster Avila. In 2005, we had so many hurricanes it was ridiculous. We exhausted the alphabet and had to start using Greek names. By the time we hit Epsilon, Forecaster Avila seemed frustrated, as evidence by this November 29 bulletin, called a discussion:

"SATELLITE WIND DATA INDICATE THE LARGE NON-TROPICAL LOW PRESSURE SYSTEM LOCATED ABOUT 730 NMI EAST OF BERMUDA HAS ACQUIRED ENOUGH CONVECTION NEAR THE CENTER TO BE CLASSIFIED AS TROPICAL STORM EPSILON . . . THE 26TH NAMED STORM OF THE **APPARENTLY NEVER ENDING** 2005 ATLANTIC HURRICANE SEASON"

Seriously, though, most hurricanes in Florida occur in August and September, as do most Category 5's. It does make sense to be prepared without panicking. Floridians must decide, first, if they will go. And, if they're going to go, they know to go as soon as they can—but also to have a plan for reentry; many beach communities have an easy way to let residents back over the bridge, because they can close access. People on the mainland have more to fear with looters or not being able to get back to their home and thus may be reluctant to leave.

Which is why, I think, we have such a rich treasure trove of hurricane lore. That is to say, how to prevent, avoid and detect hurricanes. Here's a sampling.

Ever heard of St. Elmo's Fire?

Saint Erasmus of Former, and, if you're Catholic, he's the patron saint of sailors and stomach pain. St. Elmo's Fire is a weather phenomenon that happens when there's a lot of electricity in the air, say, during a thunderstorm. The discharge of electricity produces a glow, and sailors would often see this at the top of their masts. Some sailors believe that seeing it is a warning of a hurricane. Of course, since summer is when we have many tropical storms, complete with thunder and lightning, this is inexact.

We have plenty of superstitions and other beliefs about hurricanes. For example, I've had people tell me that the reason Pinellas County—home of St. Petersburg—doesn't get hit with hurricanes is that the Indians blessed the land, or that there's a sacred burial ground here. We do get hit—Elena in 1985 was our last direct hit—but not badly. The reason has more to do with geography and where hurricanes form than belief systems, though.

Also not exactly accurate is the idea that when the sawgrass blooms in the Everglades, a hurricane is approaching. This is reportedly a Seminole belief. Sawgrass, however, blooms every fall, and August and September are when Florida has the most hurricane activity, so this, too, is inexact.

Some remarkable superstitions exist, too—such as when a cow carries its tail upright, or if an alligator makes a longer than usual bellow, or if sparrows hide under hedges or under roofs. Honestly, I've never stayed in one spot after an alligator starts to bellow to know what's a "longer than usual" bellow, and every time I walk to the corner market, there are sparrows under the roof ledge there, so these folk legends don't help me much.

You'll also find a full crop of homegrown advice on how to stop a hurricane from coming: Carry a red onion in your pocket all season and you'll survive any bad storm is perhaps one of my favorites. Note: not a Vidalia, and not a Spanish onion, a red onion. There's also storm survival lore: If you see a water spout, wave a butcher knife back and forth and the spout will break up and no storm will occur. It's always good to know that if you cut (not pull) weeds during hurricane season, they'll stay gone. I tried this. It does not work.

What does work to prevent or survive a hurricane? No one knows. While we don't know how we'll survive, we do know this: but for us, the National Weather Service wouldn't have the storm detection it does. What's more: Florida can prepare.

Say that about any state north of the Mason-Dixon line.

8

Florida Wildlife Corridor

Over the River and through the Woods

About a half hour away from Clewiston, ground zero for the Hurricane of 1928, I'm west of Lake Okeechobee in LaBelle, sitting at a diner table eating tater tots and a chicken sandwich while Carlton Ward Jr. snacks on mussels. Snacks, perhaps, isn't the right word, but he certainly isn't diving in; he's talking and tired and the mussels are almost an after-thought. The man needs to eat—he has three little kids at home and has been traveling the backroads of Florida for more than a few days—but he's too enraptured with the topic at hand: the Florida panther.

The panther's much-needed salvation has been a long time coming, but it wasn't always that way. Before Euro-Americans walked in the "New World," the panther enjoyed a much different existence. According to the Seminole, the first animal to walk the earth—by the wish of the Creator and the Wind—was the panther.

"The Creator made sure that certain animals and plants possessed unique healing powers. When the Creator touches certain things longer than normal, His powers automatically go into what He touches. He told Panther, 'When it's complete, I would like for you to be the first to walk on the earth. You are majestic and beautiful. You have patience and strength. There is something special about you. You are the perfect one to walk the earth first.'"

Europeans who later arrived in Florida did not share this sentiment. Once upon a time, the Florida panther—the Florida version of the cou-gar or mountain lion—roamed across the Southeast, but as Europeans discovered these areas and liked them every bit as much as the panthers did, these big cats found their wandering ways curtailed. Add to that our less-than-symbiotic history of killing things we fear, and couple that with farmers and ranchers upset at panthers finding their livelihood convenient alternatives to its traditional hunting patterns, and in the 1800s we were killing panthers like they were cockroaches on a wedding cake. In 1832, a bounty placed on their wild, furry heads helped drive this species to near extinction; in 1887, a five-dollar-per-scalp reward drove the knife deeper into the heart of the species.

Alongside that, as more and more people decide Florida's a way better choice than, say, Minnesota, and they're building homes here, which means clear-cutting lots of land. As a result, the panther's main food source—deer—drops from 13 million in 1850 to 1 million in 1900. By 1900, Florida panthers numbered only five hundred. Today, of the twenty-seven subspecies of panther that once roamed the eastern part of the country, the Florida panther alone now peers out from the cabbage palms. In 1950, Florida declared the Florida panther a game species, which allowed for hunting but also imposed bag limits. In 1958, the state listed it as an endangered species. In 1978, the state made killing a panther a felony. In 1992, biologists found fewer than one hundred panthers in South Florida. This alarmed biologists and conservationists, who realized that aside from our past efforts to actively kill the panther, other things were placing it in peril, too: we were turning its habitat into shopping malls and gated communities and also minimizing the ability of its food (deer, hogs, armadillos) to survive. By the time we realized we weren't making the best choices, ecologically speaking, it was almost too late—we'd reduced panther habitat to less than 5 percent of where it once roamed.

Carlton and I aren't only talking about the Florida panther, though: we've just come from a wildlife underpass off State Road 80, where he encouraged me to drop to all fours and head toward his camera trap. Above the windows in our restaurant—the down-home Forrey Grill on what may pass as the town's main drag—no fewer than five prints of Eric Enstrom's *Grace*, three replicas of Leonardo da Vinci's *Last Supper*, and a lone woman praying (Jack Garren's "Gratitude," facing down the Enstrom quintet) watch us dine. As Florida's wild areas shrank over the past half millennia, so did habitat for the Florida panther and a not-insignificant number of other fauna and flora.

Florida panthers are not that different from pumas or cougars; they're all part of the same genus, *Puma*. They used to live all over the Southeast, as far west as Arkansas—and there were other subspecies in the eastern United States. They love to eat deer. When the Europeans came and started raising livestock, though, these cats found that they enjoyed steak as much as venison, which these Euro-Americans found unacceptable. Of course, to the panther's way of thinking, those Europeans were exotic invasives taking over their land and destroying their habitat. Today, there are no other relatives of the panther in the eastern US; the Florida Fish and Wildlife Conservation Commission (FWC) says anywhere from 120 and 230 panthers remain in the wild, which is better than it was in the early 1970s, when there were only twenty.

As I work my way through my tater tots, I listen to Carlton talk and ponder the plight of the panther, which should, because of human action, be extinct. In the mid-1990s, biologists were concerned that, with so few panthers remaining, the gene pool wouldn't be great enough for the panther to ever recover. To keep the gene pool diverse, scientists brought in eight female Texas pumas, the panther's closest neighbor. The scientists reasoned that before humans destroyed panther habitat with farms, subdivisions, and highways, the Florida panther had traveled west to make new panthers with these Texas pumas. The scientists were removing the obstacles, not changing the gene pool.

Of those eight females, five of them successfully bred with the Florida panther and had a total of twenty kittens. Of those Texas pumas, five died of varying causes, and three were removed from the wild and placed in captivity once biologists thought the program was a success. Today, FWC panther team leader Darrell Land says somewhere between 120 and 230 panthers exist (not counting, he says, kittens still dependent on their mothers). It may not seem like a huge jump, but at the low end, it's a 20 percent increase in population. At the high end? The population has more than doubled.

As those numbers increase, though, another problem presents itself.

Wildlife needs space to roam, some wildlife more than others—a male panther needs several hundred miles for hunting and mating. Too many male panthers too close together not only reduces how well the big cats can hunt and mate, but the males will fight for dominance.

Ward has a network of camera traps that photograph panthers as they move between a blend of public and private land. Half of those camera traps live north of the Caloosahatchee River; he's set the other half south of the river. For years, his cameras, along with state-owned ones, documented male panthers exploring Florida ever-northward, moving out of their tiny box in Southwest Florida. The females, however, stopped on the southern bank of the Caloosahatchee River near Fort Myers. This effectively limited the big cat's range, because the males had to return to Southwest Florida to mate.

If a population expands but its habitat doesn't, it's bad news for the species—and not only panthers. Unlike alligators, who I've seen piled on top of one another, pig pile–style, large mammals like the panther need room to roam. Populations of Florida black bears, for example, need roughly 400,000 acres to flourish.[1] That presents a problem for a state that has yet to find a way to staunch the inflow of humans (almost one thousand people *per day* move to Florida, according to estimates).[2]

The houses themselves aren't a problem per se; anyone who has coyotes in their neighborhoods (which, in Florida, would be every one of us) knows that wildlife can adapt to humans—but only so much. We can put nesting platforms out for osprey, and they will use them to rear their young, but if we contaminate the water and poison their food source, they won't survive. We can create wildlife habitat in our landscape, but there's little we can do to avoid hitting a deer that jumps out at our car at night, or the possum who appears seemingly out of nowhere. Florida roadkill, as in many states, is a sad reality of human occupancy of wild areas made less wild.

In 1986, when a car hit and killed a female panther on SR 84, it was a big deal—because it was the first time state biologists had any evidence of a female panther trying to move north. And for the species to survive, the females—not just the males—must move north, so their male kittens can find room of their own to hunt and mate. But even when female panthers successfully crossed SR 84—thanks to a wildlife crossing under the I-75 portions of this road—they didn't move north of the Caloosahatchee River, which connects the Gulf of Mexico with Lake Okeechobee at about the same latitude as Fort Myers.

That's where the Florida Wildlife Corridor comes in.

The notion of a wildlife corridor isn't new—biologists in Central America created a corridor so monkeys could cross from South America to North without coming out of the canopy—but in Florida, where interstates and subdivisions wage constant war on wildlife, it's complex. A conservation easement, however, sounds more complex than it is. Simply stated, easements limit the future development rights for a property. For example, if a rancher owns 1,000 acres of cattle ranch, he can get an easement that allows the ranch to always be a ranch—even if it changes ownership—but no matter what happens, no one can develop the land for a more intense use, like a shopping mall or an "active adult community." Creating a conservation easement means the landowner gives up the higher profits he would get if he could sell the land to a strip mall developer, but the conservation easement comes with a tax break: the difference in the value of the land with full development rights compared to current development rights. That easement will stay with the property forever.

The Florida Wildlife Corridor, when completed, will form a connected network of green space and pathways that will allow wildlife, if it so desires, to cross from the Everglades to the Alabama and Georgia borders. The nonprofit organization by the same name has designated 17 million acres that could significantly change the game for Florida's wildlife by preserving green space and reopening historic migratory patterns. Wildlife underpasses allow panthers, bears, gators, raccoons—to name a few—safe egress under roads. Of those 16 million acres, more than 2,000 acres have conservation easements; another 9.5 million acres have protection of some form (parks, preserves, and other public lands). That's good news for panthers, because more room to roam means less competition, and less competition means less time fighting and more time making panther kittens.

"The greatest challenge to the Florida panther is access to habitat," Carlton tells me. "For the Florida panther to be considered recovered from the endangered species list, there needs to be three times the number of panthers there are today, distributed across two different additional populations in different parts of Florida or the Southeast."

"This," he continues, his dinner all but forgotten, "is where the Florida Wildlife Corridor and protecting a network of public and private and conservation lands throughout the Florida peninsula is really the answer for providing a path to recovery for the Florida panther, because without access to that habitat, the prospects of recovery become increasingly bleak."

That could be a grim reality.

"We lose 20 acres an hour to development," he says. "The land that is being lost to development is predominantly working agricultural land, cattle ranches, timberland, orange groves—all of which provide functional habitat for panthers and other wildlife."

The Corridor offers salvation amid the bleakness of Florida's burgeon-
ing strip-mall-and-suburb bender. Upon completion, it will connect all
the different parts of paradise. If you were to take a walkabout, you'd
end the walk with a grand sense of the wonder that is Florida, starting
in Big Cypress National Preserve, at the visitor center, which offers the
classic Florida juxtaposition: you're inches from a cypress swamp forest but also feet from US 41, a.k.a. the Tamiami Trail. You step off the
pavement and into a world of subtropical wonder: air plants cling grace-
fully to pine and cypress trees, surrounded by freshwater that's made
an achingly leisurely meander from up by SeaWorld down to the state's
lower bits. Large ferns feather out over the forest floor, sharing a limestone base pockmarked from eons of acidic rainfall with saw palmettos.
For their part, their broad, fanlike fronds, growing out of twisted arches
of trunks, offer cover for everything from squirrel to panther. Out of
the water, cypress trees blossom, their water-swollen trunks offering a
broad, stable base for the roots as they stream skyward.

The swamp is a glorious, divine place.

Farther south you'll find Florida Bay, at the crusty estuarine edge of
North America. Down here, the Flamingo visitor center is the final outpost, hemmed in from the salt of Florida Bay by some of the largest
mangroves you may ever see.

On the other side of the mangroves, paradise awaits: while you can
drive to Flamingo, the easiest way to get there is on a boat from the
Florida Keys. Paradise—at least, my paradise—is right there, across a
shallow salty bay.

If you were to follow the Corridor, you'd understand the inner work-
ings of the Everglades in reverse. As you move north, things change.
You travel across sandy limestone over rocklands, under few-and-far-
between pine trees offering shelter to birds, snakes, and lizards in the
Florida scrub, through leafy, verdant hardwood forests.

Along the path of the Corridor, near Lake Okeechobee, Carlton did
his best to persuade me to crawl toward the wildlife camera. He wanted
me to see the Corridor as a panther would as it emerged from a wildlife
underpass and Ward's camera traps get their photographs. It's tempting
to acquiesce—after all, he's giving me the chance to see something not
many Floridians will ever see—but I am no panther. A trickle of glossy
black water streams through lush, viridescent grasses, underbrush, and
trees. A pair of almost-forward-facing obsidian eyes, flecked with am-

ber, track us from not-quite-beneath the surface of the water as traffic streamed by overhead, oblivious to the diorama of survival beneath their tires. I felt vaguely Heinlein-esque, a stranger in a strange, glorious land.

That diorama played out in LaBelle, a small town east of Lake Okeechobee and south of the Caloosahatchee River, in South Florida. LaBelle, in case you haven't had the chance to visit (and most people haven't; cattle, not beaches, blanket the land in these parts), has plenty to offer Florida's future—most of it green. This wildlife underpass in LaBelle offers safe passage for the Florida panther, black bear, and other creatures that make paradise, well, paradise.

Welcome to the Florida Wildlife Corridor, a work-in-progress and labor of love for Floridians like Ward, Mallory Lykes Dimmitt, and Meg Lokey. Almost a decade ago, a cadre of dedicated Florida-philes, including Ward and Dimmitt, put together an expedition through Florida's wettest, wildest places. Their reason? They wanted to know if enough wild Florida remained to cobble together a pathway of green that would allow wildlife to safely resume natural hunting, foraging, and migrating behaviors. Those expeditions formed the nucleus of the Florida Wildlife Corridor, perhaps most widely known through Ward's photos.

But the Corridor is so much more than a photo op. Webbed together by a patchwork of state and national parks and preserves and cattle ranches, the Florida Wildlife Corridor is a spectacular example of how private-public partnerships can protect the natural environment. When complete, the Corridor will allow Florida's animals and ecosystems to exist in spite of humans.

The notion of a wildlife corridor isn't new—remember those biologists in Central America who created a corridor so monkeys could cross the land without coming out of the canopy?—but Florida has emerged as a national leader in how to create these corridors.

While the Corridor starts (or ends) 63 miles south of LaBelle, in Big Cypress National Preserve much of the land between the National Preserve and the Florida–Alabama border remains in private hands, thanks to those conservation easements, which are managed by state and federal agencies. Still other parts of the Corridor exist because nonprofits such as Conservation Florida or the North Florida Land Trust use donor money to buy land to preserve as part of the Corridor.

In these days of Weird Florida and Florida Man, the Florida Wildlife Corridor offers Floridians a point of pride. In 2021, the Florida State Senate and House of Representatives unanimously agreed to protect that point of pride, voting to create the Florida Wildlife Corridor Act, which not only formally recognized the Florida Wildlife Corridor but also codified the state's commitment to Florida's natural areas and earmarked $400 million to do just that. Florida governor Ron DeSantis signed the act. In 2023, the state legislature added almost 40,000 acres to the Corridor. Public support for the Corridor was, no doubt, bolstered by Carlton's release of the documentary *Path of the Panther* in February 2023.

Finally, Carlton tired of waiting for me to play and dropped to his knees, and—still smiling—crawled toward the cameras, which started taking photographs immediately. They only take photographs as animals emerge from the underpass, not going toward it, he explained, so as not to discourage them from using the underpasses. From eye level, the wildlife crossing looks . . . like not much: fencing that funnels wildlife to this one point, a few well-camouflaged cameras, and some vegetation around a leveled bit of riprap. You can't see any of this from the road, and most people don't even realize they're driving over one. But from on high—from 400 feet, the underpass tells a different story. It's a story of danger, death, life, and, ultimately, salvation.

Salvation. I snap my attention back to the present and what Carlton's saying about what it's like to see a panther. Not after the fact, checking the images taken the night before, but when he's out in the field, not trying to find panthers. Three times, he tells me. That's how many times it's happened to him. The Florida Wildlife Corridor could be the panther's salvation.

"This is the first time in my lifetime that there's been the opportunity for the breeding range to actually expand north of the Caloosahatchee River, and that is the first step toward establishing an additional breeding population and moving in a direction where the panther can recover into its former range throughout the Florida peninsula," he says.

Ward's referring to the day in March 2017 when biologist Jennifer Korn caught something on a state-owned camera trap: a female panther with two kittens north of the Caloosahatchee. Conservationists and journalists and biologists cheered. In 2020, another female panther made her way across the river, the third time since Carlton—or I, or many of you reading this book—have walked this earth. For the first time since its listing as an endangered species, biologists have evidence that the panther's habitat is growing, not shrinking.

I glance up at the paintings.

Grace and Gratitude.

And, not least of all, hope.

9

Archbold

How the Brooklyn Bridge Could Save the Scrub Jay

After my dinner with Carlton, I keyed on something he'd said: the Florida Wildlife Corridor was born at Archbold Biological Station. The Station attracts not only panthers but other animals you won't likely see elsewhere.

That's not hyperbole; it's truth. When I read Douglas Adams's *Last Chance to See* in the early 1990s, everything about to disappear in the book felt far away. As I step out of the car and into the scrub at Archbold, the imminence of extinction feels much closer than it did thirty years ago. Douglas Adams talked about Yangtze River dolphin and Komodo dragons, but he never once mentioned the scrub jay or the indigo snake. North of Lake Okeechobee, these creatures and their tenuous existence replace the dolphin and dragons as animals I can't bear to lose. The more I explore the Station, the more I understand how Carlton and his crew birthed the Corridor here.

Most people have probably never heard of it, but for a Florida girl bent on pulling back the veneer of the Sunshine State, Archbold is required reading. Well, required exploring. I can—and often do—rhapsodize about our stellar state park program and the state's history of preserving swaths of land, but when I tell the story of Florida, I can't leave out Archbold's story of private Florida dreams made public.

West and slightly north of Lake Okeechobee, quite near the swamps of South-Central Florida, lies a desert of sorts: the Florida scrub. Think of it as a palm-and-oak-fringed sandy desert, home to all manner of wildlife rarely found elsewhere. You'll find scrub habitat in higher elevations, and the soil tends to be well-drained, making it ideal habitat not only for scrub jays, indigo snakes, and sand skinks but also for things like shopping malls, subdivisions, and paved roads. That's why, in recent history—which is to say for as long as humans have found Florida a desirable place to live—Florida's scrub habitat has given way to development, and these animals, along with many others, have been forced out of their habitat by what we like to believe is progress. But here, at the Archbold Biological Station, the scrub remains undeveloped and pristine, an eternal preserve for the endangered animals who depend on it. Archbold Biological Station, off State Road 70 in Venus, Florida, operates as a not-for-profit research institute that concerns itself with preserving Florida's natural glory and biodiversity. It covers almost 9,000 acres of some of Florida's most endangered habitat.

That habitat exists because of an ancient beach, today called the Lake Wales Ridge. The ridge runs along the center of the Florida peninsula for nearly 150 miles, a bumpy backbone rising higher than the rest of the state's topography. When most of the Florida we know today was underwater, it was the beach, an ancient shoreline. Today, you can paddle the waterways along the ridge and pull from the sandy river bottom fossilized shark's teeth. In the Micocene era, water levels were about 82 feet higher than they are today. That meant that Florida as we know it would have been much smaller—and our beaches would have been much farther inland. But the Lake Wales Ridge remained out of reach of sea level rise. If the ridge was high and dry during the last flood, it's more so now: along peninsular Florida, the Lake Wales Ridge marks the highest elevation—312 feet at Sugarloaf "Mountain" (Florida's highest point anywhere, Britton Hill in the Panhandle, isn't much taller at 345 feet, but trust me, it's a struggle to pedal a beach cruiser up either) in Clermont, near Walt Disney World. Archbold Station's elevation isn't nearly that high, ranking from 110 to 213 feet above sea level.

But it's high enough.

High enough for what? Well, for that scrub ecosystem. It's pretty important stuff for lots of critters. As the glaciers melted some twelve thousand years ago (give or take a millennium), the Lake Wales Ridge remained out of reach of encroaching seawater, and that allowed a unique ecosystem to blossom. The ancient shoreline means today you'll find sand instead of dirt, and the higher elevation means that different sorts of animals will live safely here as opposed to anywhere else in Florida.

As of this printing, Florida boasts 195 parks, thirty-eight state-managed forests, four national forests, and one of only eleven national scenic trails. Sometimes it seems like our parks department—run by the Department of Environmental Protection—adds a park a week. But, unlike so many of the lands scooped up as part of Florida's robust public lands program, Archbold doesn't exist at the pleasure of the state legislature. The southernmost scrap of scrub remains intact and unmolested because of the Brooklyn Bridge.

John Augustus Roebling was born in Prussia—now part of Germany—in 1806. He studied as an engineer, then came to the United States in 1831, where he continued his passion: bridges. He arrived in Western Pennsylvania, where he, along with his brother and other Germans, founded Saxonburg as a farm town but then turned his attention to civil engineering, inventing wire rope and, ultimately, starting a steel cable company that made him a wealthy man. He also earned a reputation as something of a genius with suspension bridges, which were, before Roebling, unreliable in strong winds or when taxed with a heavy load. We best remember him, however, for the Brooklyn Bridge, which opened in 1883. Roebling, however, didn't live to see this spectacular feat of engineering. In 1869, before construction started, he was taking compass readings at the East River when a boat smashed into his foot. Three weeks later, he died of tetanus. His son, Washington A. Roebling, assumed leadership on the project. The younger Roebling had worked with his father and had helped design the Brooklyn Bridge. Morale among the workers, however, could have been better; bridge building wasn't the safest work around. The men would work in caissons, underwater air chambers designed for construction work, but would often get the bends (decompression sickness). After the twentieth man died, Roebling began working in the caissons himself to boost morale, pointedly staying down in the caissons longer than any of his men. Of course, he, too, got the bends, and one day in 1872 he was brought to the surface unconscious. He never worked on the bridge again, but his wife, Emily, carried out the rest of his design work. When the bridge opened in 1883, the first Mr. Roebling had died and the second lacked the health or strength to attend. Emily Roebling accompanied President Chester Arthur across the bridge. She gets little of the credit, noted only as an accessory to her husband, but without her, Manhattanites would have had to find another way to cross the East River into Brooklyn. She was but one of two great Roebling ladies that changed a nation. Her grandson, Donald—son of their son, John Augustus Roebling II—would be the one who married the family fortune with this research and preservation oasis in South Florida.

We'll get to him in a moment, but first, the Dewey Decimal System. (*Stay with me here!*) In 1895, a man named Melvil Dewey—yes, *that* Dewey, the Dewey Decimal System—founded a social club called the Lake Placid Club in Lake Placid, New York. In the mid-1920s, the Club bought a brand-new hotel in Lake Stearns, Florida, and, although it *was* brand-new, began construction on it to make it larger. They lobbied the Florida Legislature to change the name "Lake Stearns" to "Lake Placid," which it did, in 1927. They built several other outbuildings on the north shore of Lake Childs, which they also renamed Lake Placid. As Florida entered the Great Depression—and later, the rest of the country—tourists stopped coming, and on May 1, 1931, the Lake Placid Club in Florida closed. Fire ripped through the main building sometime in the 1950s, although some of those outbuildings still exist.

John Augustus Roebling II moved to Florida because he frequented the Lake Placid Club in New York and when he heard about the Florida club, he thought it would be good for his wife, Margaret. Unlike Dewey, Roebling waited to buy land; in 1929 and 1930, a few years after Florida's 1920s land boom went bust in 1926, he did buy more than 1,000 acres 8 miles south of Lake Placid. Roebling intended to build a mansion on the highest part, 213 feet above sea level. He planned to call it Red Hill.[1]

The Atlantic Coast Railroad (née Plant System) serviced the area, running alongside the edge of the Roebling parcels. Anticipating the construction and filling of the mansion with grand decor, Roebling ordered a storehouse and other outbuildings constructed near the railroad. But before he could get to the house, his wife died. He lost interest in Red Hill and remarried. (Although he did finish the buildings—at least one historian suggests he did so as a way to give work to as many men as possible, suggesting that Roebling considered this his personal WPA effort.)

So what does a millionaire do with a piece of property he no longer needs or wants? He donates it, of course. And that's where Richard Archbold and his Archbold Biological Station come into play. Archbold's grandpa was John D. Archbold, the second president of Standard Oil. The first, of course, was another John—John D. Rockefeller. Archbold sold his (relatively) small oil company to Standard Oil and determinedly worked his way up to CEO. The wealthy in America at this time weren't a huge lot, so it's no shock, really, that his grandson Richard Archbold became fast friends with school chum Donald Roebling, son of John Junior. Archbold hadn't finished college; instead, he'd opted to explore the world. He founded Archbold Expeditions while at the American Museum of Natural History, and he not only organized and led three expeditions to New Guinea in the 1930s, he also funded them.

He intended to lead a fourth expedition to New Guinea, but in 1940, the Pacific was not an ideal place for an American. That's where his buddy Donald comes into play, because the twosome talked of how Richard wanted to keep his expedition team together. Donald convinced his family to donate the now-all-but-forgotten Red Hill Estate—some 1,058 acres—to Archbold Expeditions. Well, he didn't technically donate it; he sold it for one dollar.

The caveat? Archbold Expeditions would use the land for research, which was fine with Richard, who, over time, would add more land to the reserve. Although Archbold played a part in further expeditions across the world, from the moment the Roebling family signed over the land, Venus, Florida remained his forever home.[2] When he died, he left his fortune—which is to say, the family fortune—to keep Archbold Biological Station running in the scrub.

And, oh, what a scrub it is. To the untrained eye, the scrub might not appear much more remarkable than a sandy front lawn, but once you've hiked it, you come to understand why it matters. You park in front of that old rail depot, the one that once stored the Roebling family's furniture. Today, you'll find researchers housed there, working with birds, insects, restoration ecology; think of Archbold as a Florida scientist think tank.

Surrounding the depot, the scrub waits. You set out along a trail, and the first thing you notice is the sand. It's everywhere, but you're definitely not at a beach. The creamy ecru sand belies its grainy texture, and perhaps it seems so abundant because it's a canvas with few bold strokes. The trees here—the tall ones, anyway—space themselves far apart, connected by patches of scruffy underbrush. Underneath everything, the sand lies, blanketing the limestone, a quartz-like souvenir of the last time Florida saw severe sea level rise.

It's worth mentioning that Florida citrus grows along sand like this up and down the Lake Wales Ridge, and, as Florida guru Dr. Gary Mormino once remarked to me, "you have to wonder how in the world we did it, in sand." Well, we did—often at the cost of the scrub itself. Florida's citrus belt is more of a citrus spine, and, thankfully, it ends before Archbold. Not much before, though; you can see groves lining US 27 almost up to the preserve surrounding the research station's front door.

So, at Archbold, staff scientists—as well as visiting scientists and students—collect information that helps preserve wild Florida and also helps people understand wild Florida. They don't limit their research to what you'll find on the preserve, although two of the most exquisite animals that call the scrub—specifically, Archbold Station—home live steps away from that rail depot. Meet the indigo snake and the scrub jay, and while the two aren't exactly best buddies (to snakes, most small birds are tasty little snacks), they both depend on the same sandy preserve for their existence.

Indigo snakes are hands-down the most spectacular snake in Florida, although I admit I've never seen a real one. Most likely none of us will ever get to see one in the wild. They're not blue; technically, we'd call them black, but not a flat black; indigo snakes glitter in the sun. In the Sunshine State, this violet and indigo iridescence could make Adam love a snake. One reason? They eat venomous snakes—they're immune to a rattlesnake's venom—and since rattlesnakes love the scrub as much as the indigo, well, guess what's for dinner? They're also simply lovely; remember those old cartoons of snake charmers or pictures of traveling circuses? Some sources suggest those snakes were indigos.

If they're so great, why don't we see them more? Well, indigo snakes—like rattlesnakes—live in gopher tortoise burrows, and as we built suburbs in Florida's wild areas, we used to gas gopher tortoise burrows to kill rattlesnakes.[3] This also killed indigo snakes. The other thing we did was cut down longleaf pine forests for paper, and for a snake with a scientific name that means, in part, "forest ruler" (the *Drymarchon* in *Drymarchon couperi*), well, that doesn't help. We systematically destroyed almost everywhere they call home; up by my home in Gulfport, St. Petersburg's Boyd Hill Preserve still has signs marking the edge of the indigo snake habitat, but rangers tell me the park hasn't had enough diversity to support these sparkling, friendly snakes in years.

While you can't find one in most of the places they used to live, if you're going to find one, you're likely going to find it at Archbold, because the bulk of what we know about the snake comes from research there. They have a photo of one with a reddish head—sort of the crème de la crème of indigos—on their website. If this snake stands a chance, it stands a chance at Archbold.[4]

Living near the snake—but also a respectable distance from it—the scrub jay also calls Archbold home. This scrubby area is one of the few remaining places where these jays can spread their wings. I often describe scrub jays as resembling blue jays who had been out drinking all night: a little more rough-and-tumble looking, and they don't have the spectacular markings of the more common blue jay. Despite their gruff appearance, they're docile, curious, and friendly, a combination that rarely works out for animals. In the case of the scrub jay, this is startlingly so. Nevertheless, as you walk the sandy trails at Archbold, if you can mimic the calls of the scrub jay, they will come out to greet you. I try it on one hike; I can't mimic a scrub jay, but I can call up videos of them calling to each other on my phone, and within seconds I'm surrounded by the curious blue-and-gray birds who cock and twist their heads as they try to puzzle my calls. Every one of these endangered birds has a band on its leg, because Archbold scientists pay close attention to these populations. When they realize I have nothing to offer them, they flit back to their bushes, but before they do, I'm transfixed, eyeball to feather-headed eyeball with something future generations may never see.

It's not only the rugged adorability of these birds that captivates me; it's the way they've worked out their social system. That social system depends wholly and completely on the existence of the scrub.

Archbold isn't the only scrub in Florida; at one time you could find it both along the coast and the state's interior. Walt Disney World is built on scrub, and they've preserved quite a bit of it. I first had a glimpse of it in college, when I took a course called "Identifying Florida Biota." Professor Jerry Smith had a former student who worked at the Walt Disney World Tree Farm, and she allowed us to visit. Now, if you go on the backstage tour of the tree farm today, they take you near the back side of Hollywood Studios, which is not the same place. But in the early 1990s, the tree farm was closer to US 27—a few exits west of Disney where we used to always stop and get gas when I was a kid and we were headed home—and I remember a hot trek through a sandy area, not that different from what you'll find hiking Archbold at the southern end of US 27. In either place, you can find scrub jays. Why there? Why only there? Why can't these birds live, as do other jays, in my neighborhood? Why can't they, just as their more traditional jay cousins do, thrive in my live oak and harass my cats through our sunroom window?

It's all about that social system. The scrub has few tall trees but plenty of shrubbery, which allows the scrub jays to work like this: In a colony, the birds take turns posing as sentinels—one bird stays in a tall tree while the others tend to their young, forage for food, and do other bird things. In this system, the only bird in danger is one bird, and if there's a hawk nearby, the scrub jay sounds the alarm. The rest of the colony circles the wagons and hunkers down until the danger has passed. In the case of snakes or other land-based threats, the sentinel bird has a different call, and when the sentinel sounds this call, the colony attacks the snake en masse to keep it away.

And who's a part of that social system? Scrub jays stay with their parents after they fledge; several clutches of birds will live in one colony. From a colonial standpoint, it's an Old World way of living, or, perhaps, an Italian one: several generations living under one roof, helping to keep the family going. For these birds, as it did for my family, it works.

But what doesn't work is development. Scrub jays need scrub to survive; if fires aren't allowed to burn most of the young trees in the scrub, those trees grow bigger, and the scrub jay system of survival falls apart. Similarly, if the scrub gets developed into a TJ Maxx and tract housing, the sentinel can't do its job. The scrub jay needs open space to survey, space with plenty of underbrush but not many tall trees or structures. In Florida, we're wont to fill open space, and so the scrub jay has found itself with less and less space, banished almost to extinction.

But it remains in a few places, perhaps most notably at Archbold.

And this is perhaps why the Florida Wildlife Corridor started at Archbold. The idea of a path to restoring the natural order of things began here. It makes sense; this southernmost scrap of scrub—and as vast as it seems when you're on foot in its sandy expanse, 9,000 acres isn't much—is a stronghold on the natural order of Florida, of the way it was before we arrived, before we drained and paved and built it, before we created a wild pastoral paradise in our collective memory to honor what we'd destroyed.

And it all remains because of the Brooklyn Bridge.

10

The Everglades

Not Your Average Swamp

I'm lost in the swamp, and when I almost step on a cottonmouth, my first thought is, "Of course."

Barry and I have a nasty habit of charging headlong into situations that seem like a good idea at the time. Take, for example, the driving tour of Phenix City, Alabama. We booked a tour that promised to highlight the off-the-beaten-path parts of Phenix City: the Sin City Tours. Although the website boasted a shuttle tour, the driver pulled up in a late-model sedan. He told us to get in, and for some reason, we did. The shuttle tour was for larger groups, he explained. How many, I asked, were in our group? Just my husband and myself. Only after we'd found ourselves alone with our guide driving through a dark neighborhood, talking about the Stocking Strangler, did we wonder if maybe we shouldn't have willingly climbed into a private vehicle with a man we knew nothing about. When he encouraged us to get out of the car and walk up a hill by a vacant building—ostensibly to see the site of a lynching—we said no. We refused again when he drove us to the dead center of a cemetery right by a jail and asked us if we wanted to get out. We said no. I wondered how long it would be before our families noticed us missing.

When we finally returned to our cars, I sheepishly admitted my fears to my husband. My beloved admitted he'd had the same fears. So much so, in fact, he'd chosen to sit behind the tour guide/driver because—and this is where he pulled out his large-ish boat knife, suitable for cutting line, gutting fish, or slashing the throats of murderous tour guides—he'd had the same concerns.

"Let's go on a swamp walk," my friend Sandy said. "We saw it on PBS. It'll be fun."

"It'll be fun" will likely be carved on my gravestone. Assuming, that is, anyone can find my body to bury.

We made plans to head to Big Cypress National Preserve. Sandy handled the reservations for our group of seven. Unlike every other tour in North America, this Everglades swamp walk didn't take online reservations. You had to call, no more than two weeks ahead of time. And so she did. We had our spot reserved, and we had a plan: spend the night at the Rod & Gun Club and meet for an 11:00 a.m. walk.

"Where do we meet for the walk?" I asked.

"Monroe Station," she replied.

"That can't be," I said over the phone. "It burned down. Are you sure?" Surely, walks like these would meet at preserve headquarters, or at a part of the preserve with a welcome station still in existence.

She assured me that was, indeed, what the ranger had told her. Perhaps, she suggested, there was a new welcome center there.

Monroe Station, built in the late 1920s, offered road-weary Everglades travelers an oasis along the Tamiami Trail.[1] One of six such stations, the two-story building sold fuel and other roadside comforts to travelers.[2] For a 1930s road warrior it would have been a welcome sight indeed—even today, the ribbon of blacktop between Naples and Miami feels foreboding. Years ago, about 20 miles after I left the Trail, my car's serpentine belt broke. I broke into a cold sweat picturing that happening on the Trail, with no rest areas, no gas stations, and no relief from the gators and snakes lurking the roadside ditch at night.

And the hogs. They bother me more than anything else you'll find in the Everglades.

Most people who don't spend a healthy chunk of their lives in the Florida outback have a fear of alligators and snakes. I can make, and at several dinner parties have made, the argument that Florida's real monsters are dolphins and hogs. A domestic pig—that cute little thing with its curly tail?—will revert to its wild ancestry in an alarmingly short period of time, and Florida has hogs that have run wild since Hernando de Soto brought the first head of hog on the continent here in the early sixteenth century. Some got loose, and now? Well, now Florida has wild hog terrorizing every one of our sixty-seven counties. That includes Pinellas, our most densely populated county and home to some of the world's best beaches. Apparently the pigs have good taste. Stumble upon a gator in the wild and, unless it's been fed by humans or you're threatening its hatchlings, it will get out of your way. Happen upon a wild hog and the bristly beast looks at you and thinks to itself, "Come at me, bro."

I did not want to run into a hog at the now-defunct Monroe Station or anywhere in the Everglades.

While once upon a time Monroe Station offered sanctuary from things that go snap in the night, its heyday ended in 1988.[3] That same year, the Collier Corporation transferred the title of Monroe Station to Big Cypress National Preserve. In 2000 the National Register added the shell of the building to its Historic Places. In 2016, an idiot who wanted some good photos climbed to the top of it, lit a piece of steel wool on fire, and started spinning it. Spinning, while a well-known way for painting with light used by photographers, is ill-advised for historic wooden structures in the middle of a swamp forest.

Monroe Station burned to the ground. The oasis in the middle of the remaining Everglades went up in a fierce orange puff of smoke. So when Sandy told me we were meeting at Monroe Station, it didn't make sense. Over a cannellini bean chili, safe in the suburbs of Pinellas County (hogs and all) she recited our itinerary, reminding us we'd meet at Monroe before the tour.

"We can't," I repeated. "It burned down." I then launched into a twenty-minute explanation of the history of the Tamiami Trail, the Rod & Gun Club, and Monroe Station. Sandy listened politely, then promised me, "Well, I'll double-check."

I had the feeling Sandy and her husband, Joe—a salt-weary sort of man I'd met the same time I'd met my husband, when I crewed on local sailboats—didn't believe me. We met the night before our walk at the Rod & Gun Club. After dinner on the Barron River, I asked her a third time, "Now, where do we meet tomorrow?"

Insanity, I've read, is doing the same thing over and over again and expecting different results.

"Monroe Station," came the reply.

"It. Burned. Down." I said, not quietly.

"We know," Joe told me. "We *all* know. But unless there's a fence around the whole place, we're meeting a guide there and hiking into the swamp."

There was only a fence around part of it, turns out. And our guide—or someone dressed suspiciously like one—was waiting for us. His car—

another late-model sedan, this time a Nissan—boasted South Carolina plates.

That's when I flashed back to our Phenix City tour.

"Do you have your knife?" I ask Barry. He does.

We park the car and gather with Sandy, Joe, and the rest of our group around the trunk, where, I notice, are ten long sticks. The sticks, we learn, are to pound the ground in front of us as we walk.

This makes perfect sense in swamp logic. Swamp logic is when you find yourself doing things in the swamp you'd never consider back in polite society. I would never beat the ground in front of me as I walked, say, along Clearwater Beach. Here, however, I nod (I hope) wisely and choose a stick. Our guide, a twenty-something named Ramsey who seems preoccupied with gators.

I step up to claim my dowel and listen as Ramsey talks about gators and Everglades restoration.

Ramsey tells us he plans to avoid any areas with more than a foot or two of water because the gators would be there. Now, to those of you who have never spent time in the Everglades, this probably sounds like our man Ramsey is doing a fine job of looking out for his group. However, those of you who have spent some time in any part of Florida not lined with shopping malls and subdivisions have already dismissed Ramsey as "not local." Every child who grows up in Florida knows, more than they know our state bird or state soil (mockingbird and Myakka, respectively), that there is one rule about Florida: gators are everywhere. The fact that young Ramsey wanted to avoid an area with gators—in the Everglades!—was sweet, but it would have been far sweeter coming from someone whose job it wasn't to lead groups through the swamp.

While I don't actively seek out gators, thinking we can avoid them in the largest subtropical watery expanse in North America seems impractical. My largest concern isn't gators, and I don't for a minute think his should be, either. Ramsey proceeds to tell us about a gator attack that happened less than two months ago in another area, saying that the gator likely saw the person swimming and mistook her for prey and since we wouldn't be in water like that, we shouldn't worry. I would worry less had I not only just now learned that there'd been a gator attack locally. (I later learned the "attack" was merely a bite, and the woman suffered only two puncture wounds. She didn't even let the paramedics take her to the hospital because we Florida women are hard-core. I also learned in the same news account that the Florida Fish and Wildlife Conservation Commission says the chance of being attacked by a gator is one in 3.1 million, although the odds of getting hit by an asteroid are only one in 1.6 million so really, not helping.)

"Forget the gators," I attempt to joke. "I'm more concerned about hogs."

"That's smart," he says, nodding his head and starting off into the swamp.

I follow him. There may be hogs. There may be snakes. But there also will be magic.

A few months before, a woman at one of my Florida talks raised her hand and asked me, "How can I visit the Everglades without getting bitten by a snake?" I assured her I'd visited the Everglades often and had never once suffered at the fangs of a snake. She looked skeptical; I suggested she take a stroll down a well-marked path in a cooler month.

The Glades' reputation as a wild, savage place where humans will always be the victim has, perhaps more than anything else, contributed to its destruction. A journey through it today reveals a swamp—and prairie, cypress domes, and beaches.

If you look, you'll find much written about the Everglades, and much of it, too, will have dire warnings about its future and how we've pretty much screwed the pooch when it comes to the entire system. I'm not about to tell you any of those writings are wrong—in fact, they most certainly are not; they're 100 percent correct.

What those writings fail to tell you, though, is why you should care. I think that's because we—and by "we" I mean my fellow Florida writers and naturalists—have visited "the swamp" so often we assume you know because you've been there, too. But if that were the case, why would I get questions like that one?

It's simple: we've talked about the gators and snakes and crocodiles and damn pythons so much, we've forgotten to mention the parts that reinforce immortality rather than our own mortality.

The Everglades is magic.

First of all, it's unapologetically, savagely, breathtakingly wild. You may not realize it, but Florida's one of the wildest states you'll ever visit. And no, I don't mean because of our spring break parties. Florida's wild places—truly wild, where you need more than a cell phone and a credit card to survive—exist in every pocket of the state. In his essay "The

Trouble with Wilderness" from his book *Uncommon Ground*, William Cronon gave an early method of identifying wilderness:

"Among the best proofs that one had entered a sublime landscape," Cronon wrote, "was the emotion it evoked. For the early romantic writers and artists who first began to celebrate it, the sublime was far from being a pleasurable experience."

When William Wordsworth wrote about his experiences climbing the Alps and crossing the Simplon Pass, he mentioned darkness and light and tumult and peace. He's not, as Cronon wrote, describing a casual jaunt in the mountains. The wilderness, to him and to many, was a divine experience, a way to get closer to whomever you believed God to be. But when we talk about wilderness, Cronon also wrote—and gave examples of how—people do not associate wilderness with things touched by man. Once we touch it, he posited, we change it, and therefore we do not consider it wild anymore.

This is patently untrue, and if you were to keep reading the essay, you'd learn Cronon didn't think it true, either. When I consider whether a place is "wild," I have a basic set of questions I ask. These questions don't have to have concrete yes-or-no answers; the point is to think about how closely tied to nature these places are:

How hard is it to survive here using only my wits?

Would a cell phone help me here?

Would a credit card help me here?

Without human interference, what would this place look like in a day? A week? A month? A year?

In the case of the Everglades, the answers are incredibly difficult, no, no, and even more majestic.

Even more majestic? What's so important about a bunch of swamp and trees, anyway? You'll hear people like me lose our minds when you talk about the atrocities that have been done to the Everglades, but aside from the sort of omnipresent idea that destroying nature is a bad thing, why does it matter?

Well, first of all, nothing else in the world exists that's biologically close to the Everglades, so if we destroy it, we're sending a collection of unique ecosystems to extinction. The Everglades is a designated World Heritage Site, International Biosphere Reserve, and Wetland of International Importance. Only two other places in the world have inclusion on all three of these lists. But what's in that collection of ecosystems? All kinds of stuff. It's about biodiversity: the sort of flora and fauna you'll find in the Everglades are not the sort of things you find everywhere.

Let's start by describing the Everglades as a subtropical wilderness; that's the best—and also the broadest—description. The Everglades starts near Disney World; it once stretched right to SeaWorld's front door. We drained it for farming, cattle ranching, and development, and today it's much smaller. Don't make the mistake of thinking of it only as what you will find in Everglades National Park. If we want to discuss the ecosystems that comprise the Everglades, we need to include areas that aren't part of the National Park Service, like the Corkscrew Swamp Sanctuary and the state parks bordering some of the outlying areas of the park: Fakahatchee Strand Preserve State Park, Collier-Seminole State Park, Picayune Strand State Forest, and, where we started this chapter, the Big Cypress Preserve—to name a few.

But Everglades National Park alone covers 1.5 million acres. Depending on the part of the park we're discussing, it either has a savanna or monsoon climate. A tropical savanna has a dry season and temperatures that are always above 64° (on average). So does a tropical monsoon climate; the chief difference is the amount of rainfall. The driest month happens right after the winter solstice. The Everglades gets its water not from springs but from rivers and lakes—namely, the Kissimmee River and Lake Okeechobee. During our rainy season, Lake Okeechobee overflows and, in a perfect world, would recharge the ecosystems in the Everglades. Of course, we also built farms south of Lake Okeechobee, and suburbs, so now we try and control the flow of water. This doesn't work out so well for the Everglades and, depending on the ferocity of the storm, it doesn't work out too great for the people living south of the lake, either. Everglades National Park was created to protect the ecosystems within it; the park offers, among other things, refuge for twenty rare or endangered species; forage and breeding habitat for more than four hundred types of birds; the largest mangrove ecosystem in our hemisphere; the largest continuous stand of sawgrass prairie in North America; and the largest breeding ground for wading birds in North America.

The biggest takeaway as to why we should care about whether or not the Everglades remains part of our planet is simple: it contains a collection of plants and animals you won't find anywhere else on earth. Often when we think and talk about the Everglades' ecosystems, we're referring to those inside the national park, but the Everglades includes a cornucopia of ecosystems.

Let's start with freshwater marshes, which are flooded. In those flooded area, grasses that can handle the floods grow. Sawgrass marshes have sawgrass flooded by standing water for most of the year, wet prairie, short plants and a dazzling array of plants and animals. The Everglades also has two sloughs, which you should think of as water highways. They're slow-moving water routes covered with water for eleven or twelve months out of the year. Shark River Slough is the main slough, and its water drains to estuaries. Drainage projects that benefit sugar plantations, farms, and ranches have altered and damaged this slough. The other slough is Taylor Slough, a smaller slough but the main way freshwater flows into Florida Bay. As with Shark River Slough, our drainage "fixes" have altered and damaged this slough, and by doing so we've changed the fresh and saltwater mix going into Florida Bay, which has changed the type of plants and animals that can survive there.

The last type of freshwater marsh is an alligator hole. These aren't always created by alligators; they can also be formed when peat builds up and the area catches fire and creates a hole. Gators, though, are the main reason you have gator holes. They use their snouts to clear muck off the limestone, and the water creates a hole where animals will come for water, safety, or a cool drink. Of course, the gator's waiting there, so really, well, not the safest place for little creatures.

And, of course, the Everglades has swamps. Cypress swamps—also called cypress domes or cypress balds—contain round clumps of cypress, a tree species that is fantastically water- and bug-resistant. Cypress domes grow from depressions in the limestone, the bedrock underlying most of Florida. The water here can go from almost nonexistent to several feet deep. The deeper the water, the taller the cypress tree. Shorter trees grow at the edge of the dome. Viewed from the treeline, the dome resembles exactly that: a dome. Usually you find these domes in the middle of another swamp, called a sawgrass marsh. Most of the cypress you see in the Everglades today is new-growth cypress, because the nineteenth century wasn't known for its sustainable timber practices.

While Florida has no shortage of old homes made with cypress for this very reason, one of the best things that's come out of the cypress swamp is a little fish called the gambusia. More commonly, they're called mosquitofish. Gambusia feed on mosquito larvae, and mosquito control divisions in Florida commonly use the fish for mosquito control. It can live in nominal amounts of water, which is also where mosquito larvae hang out, so you can often see our mosquito control workers bringing bunches of these fish to drainage ditches.

That's how people picture the Everglades, but there's more, such as the tropical hardwood hammocks. These are the opposite of domes; instead of being the area of deepest water, these are islands in the middle of waterlogged land. What grows on these islands are things that could not survive in the surrounding water. Hammocks have rich soil, ideal conditions for trees to grow. A hardwood hammock includes a dense collection of broad-leafed trees (as opposed, say, to palm trees, which aren't trees at all, but grasses). When we say tropical, we mean latitudes between 23.5 degrees north and south of the equator, and the equator itself. Trees here include mahogany, gumbo limbo, and cocoplum, but also live oak and red maple. Maple trees? In a swamp? Well, that's the Everglades.

Pine rocklands are also decidedly not swamp. They're a pretty rugged place, though—talking here mostly about slash pine trees growing out of limestone rock. While the tree you'll see the most of here is a pine tree, the understory will have flora endemic to pine rocklands. These areas are also great shelter for several endangered animals, like the Florida panther, indigo snake, rim rock crowned snake, red-cockaded woodpecker, and the mangrove fox squirrel, which you can see in several different places—but only in South Florida near the Everglades.

And then, of course, we have forests. Not your New England or Pacific Coast forest, but mangrove forests. Down here, mangroves come in four flavors: black, red, white, and buttonwood. Mangrove forests are also called tidal forests and mangrove swamps. Mangrove forests grow near saltwater, and the trees can handle their exposed roots being underwater. They're critical to Florida's aquaculture, too: 75 percent of South Florida's game fish and 90 percent of our commercial fish cannot survive without mangroves. Mangroves also prevent shoreline erosion by trapping sediment in their roots; this is one of the ways our barrier islands keep from washing away to nothing.

It isn't only the roots that do incredible things—fallen mangrove leaves are yummy crab food (and other bottom-of-the-food-chain creatures). Mangroves offer great hiding places for small fry, who can escape larger fish. Mangroves are the heart of Florida's saltwater ecosystem.

Speaking of saltwater, the Everglades has no small amount. Wait, you thought it was all marsh? You'll find saltwater on three sides of the Everglades. Florida Bay is contained wholly within the Everglades, and it covers over 1,100 square miles. It's shallow water, freshwater from those sloughs mixed with saltwater from the Gulf of Mexico. In that saltwater, seagrass ecosystems provide habitat for young fish and also fertile hunting ground for larger fish. Invertebrates and microorganisms live here; it's the start of the food chain for most marine life. And yes, that water that moves through the Everglades is what gives the waters of the Florida Keys its startlingly gorgeous aquamarine color—and what supports the coral reefs.

If we climb our way up the food chain, we'll quickly get to the birds. By the numbers, the Everglades has more than 350 species, some of which are migratory but many of which live there year-round. The roseate spoonbill, kingfisher, and, of course, egrets and herons are all common sights, but the Everglades is also home to the snail kite, the Cape Sable seaside sparrow, and the wood stork, all of which are endangered species.

And, of course, we have alligators and crocs down here. How can you tell the difference between them is a question I hear a lot, and the answer's pretty easy: There are a few ways, but most of them involve getting close enough to these reptiles that your knowledge could be fairly short-lived. The easiest way to tell at a distance is that crocs are gray and gators are black—not green as a certain university mascot might have you believe.

Crocs are a pretty neat thing happening in Florida, near the Everglades. Crocs live near saltwater, which in Florida means coastal mangroves. For years, Turkey Creek and neighboring waters—warmed by the cooling waters of the nuclear power plant—housed the only population of saltwater crocs. In the past few years, though, Keys residents have started spotting crocs. Randy Wayne White tells a story about fishing and seeing a saltwater crocodile: "If we hooked a fish," he asked the fishing guide, "would he try to take it?" The guide's response was, "Only if he can't find a way to knock us out of the bloody boat first."

A ranger at Everglades National Park assures me American crocs are, indeed, profoundly lazy. One man—we're going to assume he wasn't from Florida—jumped on a croc's back in Flamingo, the southern outpost in the park, and the croc merely threw him off. The man walked away with a few scratches.

Keys residents insist the saltwater crocs are not anything like their Australian cousin, describing these apex predators as almost gentle giants—but they still don't let their dogs run off leash in canal neighborhoods.

As we walk through the dome, I'm lost in shades of green, thinking about the water barely under my feet coming from up near Walt Disney World and ultimately making its way down to Key West. I'm marveling at tiny orchids growing on massive cypress trunks. I'm breathing in peaty, moist air. All of a sudden, Ramsey yells "STOP!" and puts his hand out to me. I stop and follow his hand, his index finger pointing down.

Two inches from my water shoe is a juvenile water moccasin. Coiled around herself in a pile of muck—everything here is a pile of muck—she's mostly hidden. I quickly reverse. We all stare. I snap a shaky photo. When I look closer from a respectable distance, I can see her tightly wound yellow body. She looks less than delighted to see us.

Older moccasins, Ramsey explains, will rustle their tail across dried leaves to mimic the sound of a rattlesnake. They have no desire to see humans and will do everything they can to avoid them. Younger moccasins? They're more of a danger, he says, because they haven't learned to avoid humans and their strike—and resulting bite—will often inject more venom than that of their elders.

I do not look away from the ground for the rest of the hike.

And the rest of the hike, it seems, will take longer than we'd planned. We encountered the snake as we left the cypress dome in a different direction than we entered it. Ramsey seems unwilling to double back; he wants to show us as much of the glorious swamp as he can before leading us back to quasi-civilization. Something's wrong, though. Even I, with my eyes permanently glued to the muck, can sense his hesitation. Also, it feels like we're hiking in circles, as much of a circle as one can make when there are saw palmetto and cypress keeping you from walking a straight line. We have abandoned the relatively open area of the cypress dome and are now using our sticks to bat away vines, palm fronds, and many other green things I probably could have identified in my college sophomore "Identifying Florida Biota" course but cannot now. Not for the first time in my life, I marvel at how the Spaniards made their way inland more than a mile. Florida doesn't exist in spite of us; we exist in spite of it. This is not a forgiving hike.

Out of the dome, the temperature rises quickly—we're near on 11:30 in the morning now, and even in March, the Everglades feels like early summer. We go back through a cypress dome, although not the same one, then through more palm thatch. Ramsey forages ahead; we lose sight of him, and when he returns, he's shaking his head.

"We aren't going to go that way," he says. That's when I see his stick—broken in two.

"What the hell happened in there?" I ask him. He doesn't answer, and that doesn't bother me.

He takes another "path"—I'm putting that in quotes because it wasn't a path, it was simply the least dense area of the palm forest—and comes back, looking a bit shaken.

"There was, er, an adult moccasin there. We're going to let him be," he says. "He rustled his tail on the leaves to sound like a rattlesnake."

We walk through yet another cypress dome, more palms, and, finally, Ramsey levels with us: every way out he can find will make us traverse a creek that may be several feet deep. That doesn't seem so bad.

I want to stress that Ramsey was not lost. Ramsey knew where "out of the swamp" was—he just couldn't see a way to get us there. He had a GPS and a cell phone—with a good signal. I knew—we all knew—this because before we left the safety of his Nissan, he told us where in his dry bag to find these things "in case I can't." In retrospect, I should have meditated more on that last bit.

We walked for what felt like ages. The splendor of the deep, wet, jade forest was not so splendorous the longer we walked. By noon, we didn't care about wading through water. We were hot. We were thirsty. I hadn't looked up from the ground in ninety minutes. Somewhere, back in one of the cypress domes we'd traversed, was an adolescent cottonmouth still pissed off I'd almost squished her head.

Defeated, Ramsey led us to the edge of the wilderness. At our feet lay a tea-colored canal; on the other side, a limestone gravel hunting road. We were fewer than 10 feet away from civilization; all we had to do was cross the canal. Ramsey, in what I'm certain he thought was a reassuring way, told us to look at the water level for eyes or tails. He told us the water didn't look more than 2 or 3 feet deep. One by one, we crossed the creek.

Reader, it is not to my credit that I waited until only my husband and I remained to brave the water. I wanted the gators—hogs long forgotten—to have a few humans to choose from before I took my chances. When only Barry and I remained, I handed my taller husband my pack and gingerly took a step into the creek. Two things happened at the same time: the twigs beneath my feet gave way and I felt the cold water rush up to my chest, and I screamed. I hate cold water, but what's more, there's nothing like being up to your armpits in water you can't see through.

I came out the other side just fine, of course, my husband following close behind. Safe on the gravel lane, we walked slowly, drying in the blazing sun. Ramsey admitted, somewhat sheepishly, that he was new to Big Cypress, from, I believe, Colorado, although to us, he was a hero: he may have brought us into the Everglades, but he brought us out again.

Well, not the whole Everglades. Not even the whole swamp. Most likely, we walked about a quarter mile if we count the circles. The thing is, though, whether you're thinking about the Everglades in terms of a swamp or potentially dangerous reptiles, you're almost never thinking of all of it. Every ecosystem comprising the Everglades needs the others; they're interconnected and interdependent, and damage to one ecosystem damages the whole of the Everglades.

It's an overwhelming concept—water contamination in Orlando can hurt a tarpon in Florida Bay—but when you consider the magnitude of what the web suggests for Florida, it's one of the most spectacular places on the planet.

Baby cottonmouths and all.

11

~~~~~~~~~~

The Nature Conservancy's Disney Wilderness Preserve

Mickey Saves the Everglades

Ken's bent in half, holding his iPhone under the wooden picnic table to get a photo.

"What *is* it?" he asks me.

"It's a crab spider," I tell him. Crab spiders, arguably the most adorable arachnid on the planet, aren't why I've brought him—and others in my travel group—to the Nature Conservancy's Disney Wilderness Preserve. We're fewer than 50 feet from our cars, and already the group's exclaiming at the difference in those 50 feet.

Exactly one month before I'd wandered around the Everglades, lost and narrowly escaping death by snake, I'd led a group of Florida travelers through the Preserve. I tempted them by telling them it was the only thing they can do for free with the name "Disney" attached to it. Alas, this isn't a Walt Disney World theme park, but without those theme parks, this lovely, verdant, vital expanse of wilderness wouldn't exist.

If I'd abruptly gone from "somewhat civilized" to "abject wilderness" in the Everglades, here the chasm is more severe: I go from "obnoxiously populated" to "serene solitude" in about thirty seconds. It's enough to give a person Florida whiplash, but it's a feeling every Florida explorer knows well. One minute you're stuck at a light at the Dollar Tree/Wal-Mart intersection, and the next—literally, the very next one—you're easing your car along Scrub Jay Trail, and for a moment you wonder if you've stepped through a portal into another world, because the Wal-Mart world and this one cannot possibly share the same planet.

And yet they do.

You're in a grassy expanse of pine and scrub, which is to say you've discovered a Florida-style prairie, and if you were to keep walking away from the Wal-Mart, if you had enough food and water and mosquito repellent, you would ultimately reach Lake Okeechobee. You're dangerously close to Walt Disney World, but at the same time, you're in the wild.

And the only reason this part of the Florida frontier exists as wilderness is thanks to the much-maligned Walter Elias Disney.

While many of my Florida colleagues disparage the empire of the mouse and decry the various sins of The Walt Disney Company—and I won't deny the company must answer first to its shareholders, not Old Florida—I've long admired the more benevolent aspects of the Walt Disney World corporation, and try as I might, I cannot blame it for the downfall of Florida or the Everglades. To find the real culprit, look no farther than your local diner.

See, long before Walt decided to build the Happiest Place on Earth on the edge of the northern Everglades, cattle ranchers decided this wet, empty land would be a delightful place to raise cattle. Cows need water, and lots of it. Love hamburgers? A half-pound burger takes almost 1,000 gallons of water to get to your table, and where better to get that water than one of the wettest places on the planet, an area so pockmarked by lakes and creeks that a rancher would scarce worry about watering his cattle?

If this worked well for the ranchers and the hungry meat-eating masses, it proved far less than ideal for the landscape; ranching isn't the worst thing for the land, but the strain of growing grain in an area not meant to grow grain, coupled with the burden of all the methane-related waste, started to tax this part of the Everglades.

If you're thinking, "Hey, wait, the Everglades are in *South* Florida," allow me to clarify: Everglades *National Park* is in South Florida, and the 1.5 million acres it protects represents but a fraction of the original Glades, a magical web of interconnected, interdependent ecosystems. That web—the true, original Everglades—begins near SeaWorld, which lies northeast of Walt Disney World and slightly more than 20 miles due north of a piece of land once called Walker Ranch. You can drive it in under an hour, and if you really wanted to, you could walk it in a hearty eight hours. Once upon a long time ago, though, you could paddle it.

And even though it's closer to SeaWorld than it is Everglades National Park, Walker Ranch is indeed part of the Everglades: the Upper Kissimmee River Basin, the brain of the Everglades.

The interconnected web of ecosystems that comprises the Everglades isn't simply interconnected, it's interdependent, with changes at the headwaters ultimately impacting the coral reefs in the Florida Keys.

Starting more than five thousand years ago, long before Europeans landed in Florida in the early sixteenth century, feeder waterways trickled from the northern edge of the watershed into sub-basins with lovely names like Shingle Creek or Boggy Creek (the Upper Kissimmee has eighteen sub-basins, or shallow bowls within a larger, shallow bowl). Slowly, ever so slowly, they would move ever-south, over cypress forest and scrub, flowing into the lower Kissimmee River basin, which in turn would drain into Lake Okeechobee—which wasn't the proper lake as you may think of it today but a large, shallow basin. Throughout the year, but most of all in the summer, Okeechobee would tip the water out over its south shore, where it would spread out in wide, shallow sheets and move over sawgrass, pine rockland, subtropical savanna, and hardwood forests, ultimately slipping through a tangle of mangrove forest and off the edge of the continental United States. From there, it would join Florida Bay and nourish sea grasses and coral reefs. The drop of rain that fell into Shingle Creek would, one day, pass through the gills of clownfish as it sheltered in an anemone. In Disney terms, the water that rained on the forest where Bambi lived would one day make its way to Nemo's home. Along the way, of course, it would absorb various things as it flowed over the earth and deposit those things along its route to the sea.

At least, that's how it worked when Europeans first "discovered" it, but once cattle ranchers moved to Central Florida, the grasses, pines, and wetlands gave way to nonnative grasses (for grazing) and drained areas (for pasture.) Fertilizer and cow manure made its way to the waters draining ever southward toward what little remained of the Everglades. DDT and arsenic, the latter of which ranchers dipped their cows into in an attempt to control cattle fever tick, starting following the water into the Everglades in the 1910s.[1]

Tons of cow manure, fertilizer to grow grass for the cattle, and pesticides—along with arsenic dip and other toxins—at the headwaters run into the waters that feed the Kissimmee River, which drains into Lake Okeechobee, the water from which feeds the Everglades as we know it today, where it flows off the edge of North America into Florida Bay. Since Euro-Americans arrived in Florida more than five hundred years ago, cattle ranching has impacted the system—in addition to development, channelizing the Kissimmee River, attempts to drain the lower half of the Everglades system, draining Lake Okeechobee by altering the course of rivers and forcing them to connect to the lake, and agriculture south of Lake Okeechobee have all chipped away at the elegant system. Cattle ranching, it might seem, is the least of the worries for the Everglades, and while many modern Florida ranchers do use more sustainable practices, cows grazing in the Kissimmee River floodplain have historically impacted (and continue to impact) the health of the system.

While western artists such as Frederic Remington painted and bronzed images of the western cowboy, it's Florida, not Montana or Texas, that has the longest history of cattle ranching in the United States. Cow historians suggest that Spanish explorer Ponce de León first brought Andalusian cattle to Florida near Charlotte Harbor in 1521 via the Caribbean, although these long-horned cows, along with some later brought by Don Diego del Maldonado in 1540, escaped into what are now the Charlotte[2] and Pensacola[3] areas of Florida, respectively.[4] The first actual ranching began in the mid-1560s, when Pedro Menéndez de Avilés founded St. Augustine and had more cattle brought from Spain. Ranching flourished in Florida, with Indians also raising cattle, and when the Civil War began, Florida supplied both the Union and the Confederacy with more beef than any other state or territory. Because of its cattle industry, Florida recovered more easily than most southern states after the war, as ranchers could trade cattle for Spanish doubloons in Cuba.

In 1700, the Spanish territory included thirty-four ranches, mostly in North Florida, and over the next century, the Seminole Indians would become the primary ranchers in Florida. Cattle ranching in the Kissimmee River Valley began in the 1860s, when the earliest Euro-American families moved to the area.[5]

They settled first in an area they called Kissimmee Island—south of Lake Kissimmee, west of the as-of-yet straightened and ruined Kissimmee River, north of Lake Istokpoga, and east of Lake Arbuckle. With intense seasonal swelling of the Kissimmee, it certainly must have felt like an island.

In 1883, the city formerly known as Allendale incorporated as Kissim-mee, and developer Hamilton Disston made it his base of operations for his grand plans to drain the Everglades. While his drainage effort largely failed, he'd opened Pandora's box, and the area continued to grow in the hope of conquering the land. By 1902, a WPA history of Osceola County notes that "large herds of cattle grazed over level land."[6] In the following couple of decades, those chasing Disston's drainage dream—for what-ever reason—drained 50,000 acres of the Everglades in the Upper Kis-simmee Valley. The Upper Kissimmee River Valley starts near SeaWorld at Shingle Creek and ends near State Road 60 near Lake Kissimmee.

By 1925, loggers with the Everglades Cypress and Candler Lumber Company—of the Coca-Cola Candlers—began moving in. What long-leaf pines they didn't take, turpentine mining practices—which prey on pine trees—did. What had been a swampy celebration of life, home to black bears, panthers, red-cockaded woodpeckers, and countless other animals became flat and diminished woodland. The turpentine industry ceased operations in the 1940s, but the logging continued into the 1980s.

As cattle ranching grew, other changes, too, wore down this part of the Everglades: The seasonally swollen Kissimmee River, more a shal-low, wide floodplain than a well-defined river, would not do; ranch-ers dug trenches in an attempt to drain the water off pastureland. The grasses growing here, too, changed, as ranchers tore out native grasses and plants so they could plant nonnative plants for grazing.[7]

Even that, though, would have been preferable to tract houses and shopping malls, which is precisely the direction the Walker Ranch prop-erty seemed headed in the 1980s.

What remained of Walker Ranch was slated to become a golfing sub-division, with six golf courses and nine thousand homes. In 1978, the Candler family transferred the deed within the family for a dollar, but in 1987, the family sold it again—this time for $2.4 million, to David L. Walker.

In 1965, The Walt Disney Company—in reality, mostly shell compa-nies with names like Latin-American Development and Management Corp., Ayefour, Tomahawk Properties and M. T. Lott Co.—started buy-ing land for "Project X" in Florida. Irlo Bronson, a Florida congressman, sold slightly more than 8,000 swampy acres to Disney for one hundred dollars an acre.[8] Disney tried to buy Osceola County cowboy Oren Brown's land, which included not only ranchland but part of the Reedy

Creek swamp, for its soon-to-be subtropical empire. Brown, who—by the end of his life would serve seven terms on the Osceola County Commission and own a café legendary for raucous political debates—refused. The amount remains disputed; Brown said the rumored $4.2 million offer for 6,750 acres was highly inaccurate—the operative word here being "high."

Adjacent to Brown's property, both the South Florida Water Management District and the Army Corps of Engineers, neither of whom hold the best conservation records, had already approved permits that would allow a developer to build three thousand homes on the BK Ranch property.[9]

These ranches, one by one, were going to be subdivisions.

Each house would be one more nail in the Everglades' coffin.

Disney bought Walker Ranch for $20 million in 1992,[10] but years of degradation had brought the land to its knees. Overall, it spent almost $50 million to undo 150 years of logging, draining, and other indignities to this piece of the Everglades.

In 2014, Disney added another 3,000 acres near Walker Ranch. The company spent $11.5 million for the land near Mira Lago in Poinciana.[11]

Finally, in 2019, fifty years after Disney's initial offer for his land and more than a quarter century after his death, The Walt Disney Company bought the last bit of Brown's land, 1,575 acres, for $11 million. They'd purchased the adjacent BK Ranch property—965 acres for $23 million—a month earlier.

Between the Nature Conservancy and five different governmental agencies (the US Fish and Wildlife Service, Army Corps of Engineers, Florida Department of Environmental Protection, Florida Fish and Wildlife Conservation Commission, and the South Florida Water Management District), the Nature Conservancy's Disney Wilderness Preserve set about taking that degraded pastureland and restoring it to its rightful place as a functioning part of the Everglades. The land amount grew to include land paid for by the Greater Orlando Aviation Authority and Universal Studios, but the bulk of the funding came from The Walt Disney Company.[12]

Of course, this wasn't a wholly altruistic move, which Disney detractors will surely mention: Disney used this property as mitigation to develop its town of Celebration, which included destroying about 500 acres of wetland. It's worth mentioning, however, that those acres were scattered throughout a larger area, and while in a perfect world no one would destroy any wetlands, we don't live in a perfect world, and in this rare instance, the Everglades got the better end of the deal.

Disney turned the property over to the Nature Conservancy (TNC), who—assisted by millions of Disney dollars—restored the land as closely as possible to its pre-Euro-American state. Gone are cow pastures; instead, the land supports longleaf pine, cypress, and saw palmetto. Instead of cattle-ranching families, the land has breeding pairs of red-cockaded woodpeckers. Scrub jays, endemic to Florida and wildly endangered, thrive here. Wood storks nest here, taking advantage of freshwater pools to raise their young. The man-made canals have disappeared; instead, the limestone under the soil soaks in water like a chalky sponge, purifying it on its journey down to the Floridan Aquifer. When rains saturate the ground, the excess meanders along its ancient route toward the sea, flowing over not poisoned land, but unfertilized loamy sand and soil touched by nothing more dangerous than dead leaves and felled branches.

The Nature Conservancy reintroduced fire to the landscape, part of a necessary cycle for the land to function properly.

The Disney Wilderness Preserve opened November 1, 1999.[13]

Today, as Carlton Ward pointed out, you can enter the Disney Wilderness Preserve and find a path to Lake Okeechobee. Not easy terrain for humans, but for panthers, bald eagles, indigo snakes, gopher tortoises, and some forty other endangered species, it's a walk in the park.

12

Marjory, Marjorie, and Marjorie

Florida's Founding Mothers

The Florida Studies MLA program at USF St. Petersburg is not your average master's program. It is nothing like an MBA or an MFA; Florida Studies people are a breed unto themselves. One fellow alum describes us as all living on the Island of Misfit Toys. We have bizarre debates—heated, passionate affairs—not only about the things you might expect, such as the best freshwater springs or favorite type of seafood, but things like whether or not our parks should be removing Australian pines, whether or not Disney saved Central Florida from overdevelopment, and which sixteenth-century explorer is the "best." These are things over which friendships end in our world.

Two of my classmates, Emily and Theresa, started an imaginary debate between Marjory Stoneman Douglas, Marjorie Kinnan Rawlings, and Marjorie Harris Carr. While I cannot recall the loftier points of the many après-class arguments at the Tavern, I do remember arguing passionately from the perspective of Marjorie Kinnan Rawlings.

I'd wager many of you reading this associate Marjory Stoneman Douglas with the Everglades and have heard of—if not read—*The Yearling*; perhaps fewer of you know who Marjorie Harris Carr was. That's OK; you're about to learn, among other things, how she saved us from being sheared off from the rest of North America.

But let's back up. Who were these women, really, and how did they make Florida spectacular?

Let's start with Marjory Stoneman Douglas, only because she was born first, in 1890, in Minnesota. She came to Florida in 1915, after the end of what the National Park Service calls a "calamitous marriage." She was lucky enough to have a father who happened to publish the *Mi-*

ami Herald, and she started writing for the paper, first on the society pages, then the editorial pages, eventually becoming the writer of note for South Florida.

Most people associate Marjory Stoneman Douglas with "saving" the Everglades, or at least trying harder than perhaps any one other individual ever has. The Rivers of America series published her book about the Everglades, *River of Grass*, in 1947. Here's a fun fact about the book: Initially, the publisher wanted a book about the Miami River, but that didn't interest Douglas. She wanted to write about the Everglades, although she knew full well it wasn't a river at all but a broad, shallow expanse of freshwater drifting south over the edge of Florida. She used a bit of creative license and wrote about it anyway, calling it a "river of grass." Her autobiography, published in 1990, is titled *Voice of the River*, because that's what she did: she gave voice to the Everglades. Without Marjory Stoneman Douglas, the Everglades as we know it would likely not exist. People refer to this tiny lady—she really was quite tiny—as the "Grande Dame of the Everglades."

If you've visited the Everglades, you may have stopped at the Ernest Coe Visitor Center. Ernest Coe was the man who created the idea of Everglades National Park—he drafted the proposal to create a national park in the lower part of the Everglades. He recruited Marjory Stoneman Douglas to help him preserve this part of Florida's frontier.

Many people don't realize that Douglas wasn't a huge fan of venturing *into* the Everglades. She described them as "too buggy, too wet, too generally inhospitable" for her tastes. This did not mean she saw no value in them, however, and she quickly became the Everglades' perhaps most notable advocate. She fought tirelessly to preserve as many buggy, wet, and inhospitable inches as she could find. Her work included everything from writing a book about the Everglades to founding Friends of the Everglades, a conservation group dedicated to stopping a private airport in the Big Cypress area of the Everglades. She rallied against Big Sugar, real estate development, and the Army Corps of Engineers—all of whom contributed directly to the decimation of the Everglades.

There is no one act we can point to and say, "This. This saved the Everglades." The reality is, the Everglades remain in constant peril, assaulted on all sides by cattle ranching, development, sugarcane and other farming practices, and our own ignorance. Not to bring anyone here down, but the reality of it is we are likely harming the Everglades today in ways we don't yet realize. One Everglades restoration program was to bear Douglas's name, but it was so watered down by politics and such that she asked her name be removed from the plan.

With all those things and a history of humans decimating the Glades, there isn't one thing any one person or agency can do to "save" the Everglades. Douglas's contribution was far greater than any one thing: she brought an awareness of what it meant to have an Everglades, of what it did, to Florida, and to America. Before her, we regarded the Everglades as nothing but a swamp to be reclaimed. Think of her as the Rachel Carson of the Everglades, with more hands-on activism.

Jack Davis wrote *An Everglades Providence*, which not only tells the story of the Everglades but Douglas's story as well. I asked him what ten things you should know about her, and this is what he told me.

1. She was a lifelong feminist, not simply a suffragist. She also championed racial justice.
2. At heart, before anything else, except maybe being a feminist, she was a writer, and a beautiful and skilled one.
3. She was funny. At a 1983 hearing she attended, where she was the only one opposing draining another tract of the Everglades-turned-suburb, the crowd booed her. Now, remember, she was an itty-bitty woman, and by 1983 she was ninety-three. Instead of being a frail old lady, however, her response to the booing was simply, "Can't you boo any louder than that?" She also told them, "Look. I'm an old lady. I've been here since eight o'clock. It's now eleven. I've got all night, and I'm used to the heat."
4. She was relentless about proper grammar.
5. She never drove a car. I'd also like to add that her home had no electric stove—which is no big deal, because lots of people cook with gas—and no air conditioning. Note that I didn't say "no central air conditioning" but no air conditioning *at all*. In South Florida. Where she lived. All year. Even August.
6. She was wicked smart, with an expansive mind revealing an acumen in science, literature, history, and the human character.
7. A five o'clock daily cocktail was one secret to her longevity. And it worked: she lived to 108. She drank a blended Scotch whiskey called Desmond & Duff, but when I looked for some, I saw the price of a bottle cost more than $150, which is, to me, crazy.

I mean, it's a *blended* whiskey. That may have been why she limited herself to one a day. As to her longevity, there may have been more to it than the Scotch . . .

8. Keeping an active mind until the end—reading, writing, staying current with news events—was the main secret to her longevity.
9. She was a champion of social justice, not merely a champion of the environment.
10. She cared as much about people as wildlife.

In her first passage in *River of Grass*, Douglas did a phenomenal job of explaining why the Everglades mattered *beyond* the Everglades. I find it to be her most enduring quote:

"There are no other Everglades in the world. They are, they have always been, one of the unique regions of the earth, remote, never wholly known. Nothing anywhere else is like them; their vast glittering openness, wider than the enormous visible round of the horizon, the racing free saltness and sweetness of their massive winds, under the dazzling blue heights of space. They are unique also in the simplicity, the diversity, the related harmony of the forms of life they enclose. The miracle of the light pours over the green and brown expanse of saw grass and of water, shining and slow-moving below, the grass and water that is the meaning and the central fact of the Everglades of Florida. It is a river of grass."

If Marjory Stoneman Douglas was the voice of the land, Marjorie Kinnan Rawlings captured and amplified the voice of Florida's people.

Rawlings was born in 1896 in Washington, DC; she arrived in Florida in 1928 with her then-husband, Charles. They purchased a 72-acre farm in Cross Creek, near the Ocala National Forest. They lived roughly 18 miles southeast of Gainesville. Well, mostly she did—Charles, it seemed, was not as besotted with Florida's outback as his bride.

Rawlings's best-known work is *The Yearling*, written in 1938 and still considered a classic. *The Yearling* tells the story of a young boy who adopts an orphaned fawn. Her story transcended Florida with its universal themes, and in 1939 Rawlings won a Pulitzer Prize for it. In 1946, MGM made it into a film, which catapulted Rawlings into the limelight.

The Yearling may have made her famous, but it is by far not Rawlings's best gift to Florida. That came with her other work. See, once she moved to Florida, she found herself enchanted with the people in this primitive part of the state. Because she was a writer, this translated into a treasure trove of material for her. Rawlings had already enjoyed success as a writer; she had worked as a writer for the *Louisville (KY) Courier-Journal* and the *Rochester (NY) Evening Journal*. She also had written a series of poems called *Songs of a Housewife*.

Long before *The Yearling* brought her fame, she'd evolved from a poet and feature writer into something of a folklorist, and she developed a keen interest in the locals and their lifestyles. Her hunger for learning about local culture wasn't satisfied with her few neighbors, so in 1931 she moved in with Piety Fiddia and her son Leonard, who lived east of her in a scrub area. They taught her local ways, and also survival skills for living on the Florida frontier. For the Fiddia family, one way to survive was by making moonshine. In 1933, Rawlings published *South Moon Under*, a novel based on her experiences.

One of the truest things I believe Rawlings ever wrote about Florida is this. After her time in the scrub, she sent a letter to her mentor and editor, Max Perkins. In it, she wrote, "The scrub, as a matter of fact, has defeated civilization."

I don't know if that's true; the scrub, I think, makes for a different *sort* of civilization, one that follows its own rules. Rawlings, of the three Marjories, came latest in life to Florida: She was thirty-two. I moved to Florida when I was seven, and although I know I am not a true native, I cannot imagine calling any other state home. It seems to me the older people are when they move to Florida, the less likely they are to truly adapt to the most severe parts of the state. That's by no means a judgment of people who arrived here later in life; I'm suggesting Rawlings had to work very, very hard to be able to understand her neighbors. Remember, she was born in Washington, DC, which wasn't, even then, a wilderness—at least, not in the traditional sense. I can't speak for political animals. However, in every piece I've read of hers, she treats her Floridian neighbors with respect. She does not belittle their ways, which certainly must have seemed foreign to her, and the way she handled her subjects discourages judgment. It is rare, especially today, in a world where it's amusing to the rest of the world to mock our state, to see a northerner—a Yankee, if you will—treat Florida folkways with respect rather than disdain. She showed the world we were more than uneducated hillbillies. Her collection of stories about her time at Cross Creek, called, appropriately, *Cross Creek*, came out in 1942, and, in my opinion, it makes for a far more engaging read than *The Yearling*.

I'm as besotted with Rawlings as she was with Cross Creek, and if, at the end of this passage, you remember anything of her, remember these ten things.

1. Rawlings used an inheritance from her mother to buy Cross Creek.
2. She loved to cook. Her book, *Cross Creek Cookery*, contains her Florida recipes—and those of others—for everything from ice box cake to gopher tortoise. Her thoughts on entertaining, too, were well-documented in this book. "Better a dinner of herbs," she quotes Proverbs near the end of her cookbook, "where love is." She also cautions that "the mother or wife who grumbles over the planning and cooking of meals taints the very vitamins."
3. She struggled with alcohol. Her papers, available at the University of Florida, are filled with correspondence with her second husband, Norton Baskins; they indicate she had a drinking problem. Her premature death—she died at fifty-seven—came from a cerebral hemorrhage, not uncommon in severely heavy drinkers. These documents also indicate she battled depression and had what researchers refer to as an "uneven" personality, mirrored in her writing.
4. She befriended Zora Neale Hurston, and the two visited. When visiting Rawlings, however, Hurston slept in the maid's quarters, because, of course, Hurston was Black and Rawlings was not.
5. Rawlings had a complicated relationship with race. A writer would later describe her as a woman who would champion the cause of Black people in the abstract but curse them in person. Rawlings described a close relationship with her Black maid, Idella, but also was known to use racial slurs.
6. In 1941 she married for the second—and final—time a hotelier from Ocala, Norton Baskins. They had a "weekend marriage"; she remained mostly in Cross Creek, and he lived in St. Augustine, where he remodeled an old, large home into the Castle Warden hotel, which is currently Ripley's Believe It or Not. When asked about Rawlings's influence in the hotel, he once told a guest, "You

do not see Mrs. Rawlings' fine hand in this place. Nor will you see my big foot in her next book. That's our agreement. She writes. I run a hotel."

7. She used her money from *The Yearling* to buy a beach cottage on Crescent Beach, by St. Augustine.

8. One of her favorite people was a woman she called GeeChee, so nicknamed by Rawlings because she was part of the GeeChee people. GeeChee was her maid, and her boyfriend was in prison. When he was released, Rawlings brought him to live with GeeChee at Cross Creek, but he started threatening Rawlings, so she made him leave. GeeChee stayed on with Rawlings, much to her surprise and initial delight. However, GeeChee soon started drinking heavily, and Rawlings eventually sent her away as well. This, Rawlings said, broke her heart.

9. One of the people featured in *Cross Creek*, Zelma Cason, was a woman Rawlings considered a friend. Cason sued her, though, for invasion of privacy for the way Rawlings depicted her in *Cross Creek*. The courts awarded Cason one dollar.

10. Her home is now the Marjorie Kinnan Rawlings Historic State Park. She left most of her land to the University of Florida, and in return they named a dormitory after her—Rawlings Hall, in the middle of campus.

Although she said plenty about Florida's people in the way she wrote about them, her love for her piece of paradise bound her to Florida. I believe she sensed the same respect for the land in her neighbors, which is why she treated them with respect in her writing. My favorite Rawlings quote tells us how she, and her neighbors, saw her relationship with Florida.

"Who owns Cross Creek? The red-birds, I think, more than I, for they will have their nests even in the face of delinquent mortgages. It seems to me that the earth may be borrowed, but not bought. It may be used, but not owned. It gives itself in response to love and tending, offers its seasonal flowering and fruiting. But we are tenants and not possessors, lovers, and not masters. Cross Creek belongs to the wind and the rain, to the sun and the seasons, to the cosmic secrecy of seed, and beyond all, to time."

The last of our three Marjories is perhaps the least known of the three, although she's equally worthy as the others of recognition. Marjorie Harris Carr is the "baby" of our group.

She wasn't born until 1915, in Boston. Unlike the other Marjories, she moved to Florida when she was three and grew up in Bonita Springs. In 1936, she earned her bachelor of science in zoology at Florida State College for Women. Today, we know this school as Florida State University. In 1937 she married Archie Carr, but she remained a working scientist. Although Archie made quite a name for himself, and although in Florida we know her, I would dare say this lady is not well known outside of Florida, which is a shame. She has no *River of Grass* or *Yearling* that folks in Idaho can read.

Few readers will have heard of the Cross Florida Barge Canal. You may have heard of it, but you have never floated on it. That's because Marjorie Harris Carr stopped it. It would have been a canal that cut across the center of the state. It would have forever altered the flow of the Ocklawaha River, prevented wildlife migration, and made South Florida an island. It would have been, simply put, one of the worst environmental decisions in our state's history.

The canal had its beginnings in the 1820s, but it really wasn't practical. Technology and population made it more practical in the 1930s, and it was one of the New Deal projects slated for Florida. The plan was to cut a canal across Florida, starting at the mouth of St. Johns River at the Atlantic, at Jacksonville, across the state and south to Crystal River and the Gulf of Mexico. It would have—I can't stress this enough—made everything south of there an island. Six thousand men cleared 4,000 acres, cutting down oaks and longleaf pines, which are now quite rare almost anywhere in Florida, and driving out Florida black bears and other wildlife. The only thing that stopped the canal was Congress, who cut funding not out of any grand concern for the environment but to punish FDR.

JFK revived the canal in the 1960s, and although the Army Corps of Engineers found it impractical for reasons of economics, they quickly remedied that by deciding the "land enhancement" value of the project suddenly made it more feasible.

Carr, who had fallen in love with the Ocklawaha River and was devastated by the plans to dam it as part of the Cross Florida Barge Canal, used a combination of her scientific background and grassroots activism to get people enraged about the project. With the help of a group called the Florida Defenders of the Environment, she stopped the project two presidents later. She pushed and pushed until Nixon halted construction. Today, the only thing she didn't accomplish was removing a dam that blocked the Ocklawaha River. If you drive north on Interstate 75, you see the Marjorie Harris Carr Cross Florida Greenway. That's a remnant of the canal, but instead of being filled with water, it's filled with plant life.

Peggy MacDonald wrote the book on Marjorie Harris Carr. It's titled, appropriately, *Marjorie Harris Carr: Defender of Florida's Environment*. I asked Peggy what ten things people should know about Carr, and she said everyone should know the following:

1. She graduated Phi Beta Kappa from Florida State College for Women in 1936.
2. Marjorie Harris Carr worked as a scientist in a time when women were expected to resign from their careers upon marriage. She didn't teach science, or work in a Good Housekeeping lab, either. She was a field scientist.
3. She was the nation's first female federal wildlife technician, but was fired because she was a woman.
4. In 1942, she received a master's of zoology from the University of Florida when it was still officially all male.
5. She and her husband, sea turtle conservation biologist Archie Carr, had five children together.
6. The Marjorie Harris Carr Cross Florida Greenway is named after her. It is made up of the lands that would have become the Cross Florida Barge Canal had she not stopped it.
7. She cofounded Florida Defenders of the Environment (FDE), which still exists. In recent years, they've filed a lawsuit to force the Florida lawmakers to use Amendment One funds as the voters intended them spent instead of on nonconservation expenditures.
8. Marjorie Carr and the Gainesville Garden Club led the campaign to make Paynes Prairie Preserve a state park.
9. Carr and FDE stopped the Florida Department of Transportation (FDOT) from building a Tampa–Jacksonville turnpike that would

have gone through Paynes Prairie and other environmentally sensitive lands.

10. She and other UF colleagues stopped UF and FDOT from draining Lake Alice to build a four-lane cross-campus throughway and two-thousand-car parking lot at the lake.

Although Harris wrote no book to which we can look for inspiration, she did leave Floridians with inspiration in her words:

"I am an optimist. I also believe that Floridians care about their environment. If they are educated about its perils, if they are never lied to, they will become stewards of the wild places that are left."

These women shared more than a name. They were all enlightened women who bucked the ideal of what a woman of the time should do, from frontier woman, to a newspaper reporter who refused to confine herself to the society pages, to an environmental activist who took on the Army Corps of Engineers.

13

Emateloye Estenletkvte

The Most Spectacular Florida Woman You Never Heard Of

Women are never so strong as after their defeat.
ALEXANDRE DUMAS

While there's no doubting the three Marjories all had enduring positive impact on Florida, there's one woman whose name everyone should know—and almost no one does. Like so much of Florida's history, her story isn't taught in Euro-American schools—but it should be.

When Floridians heard about the signing of the Declaration of Independence, they burned John Hancock and John Adams in effigy in the St. Augustine town square, and for almost 250 years, historians have not forgiven us, writing the Sunshine State out of early Euro-American history, leading folks to believe we came late to the colonial party (we seem to exist in a post-Enlightenment world only) when, in fact, Florida's been part of the global party since the Renaissance.[1]

But enough about how historians have eschewed Florida history in favor of colonial history—let's talk instead about how those same historians, and many Florida ones, have ignored perhaps the most important woman in the world.

Broad statement? Perhaps. But stay with me. And let's take a trip to the middle of the Everglades, where I sit in a pleasant, air-conditioned, modern building, across from Paul Backhouse, who is not what I expected.

First of all, he's white. Quite white. He's elegant and British—one part Hugh Grant, one part Indiana Jones, zero parts Seminole. When I asked the head of public relations for the Seminole Tribe of Florida to put me in touch with someone who could speak to the Tribe's remarkable history, I expected that representative would be a member of the Tribe, but—as with so many things I thought about the Seminole prior to this meeting—I was wrong.

So here I sit, in the middle of the Everglades, sitting across from a devastatingly British man with a delightful accent.

I next realize this meeting won't be quite what I expected roughly three minutes after I sit down.

"What's the relationship between the Calusa, the Timucua, the Seminole, and other tribes who have lived in Florida?" I ask, drawing on my graduate education in Florida Studies (which included zero seminars on non-Euro Floridians) and two solid units of Florida history from fourth and seventh grades, all of which mistakenly taught me the Seminole are a blend of runaway slaves and runaway Indians from other tribes. That education also taught me that the Tribe was "new"—as in, not here before the 1700s.

Paul, being British, received no such version of history.

At my question, he blinks and stares at me as blankly as perhaps only an Englishman can, blinks again ever so briefly, then answers: "Those are just words Europeans gave the Tribe. They don't mean anything to them," he tells me. The visual that accompanies five centuries of Euro-American history shattering around you is far more glamorous than the reality. I stare at Paul and realize that everything I'd learned, I'd learned from Europeans. Euro-Americans, to be precise, with something to gain by remaining blind to reality. I shiver in the artificially cold air while the brutal sun of the Everglades pulses against the windows.

We talk. Paul gently disabuses me of most of my ideas about the Seminole Tribe, and I leave wanting only to know more. Over the next year—which, admittedly, is not long enough to understand an entire culture but is also, most assuredly, long enough to understand that we Euro-Americans have gotten almost everything about Florida's first humans laughably, heartbreakingly, tragically wrong—I make several treks down to the Seminole Tribe of Florida's Tribal Historic Preservation Office, or THPO. The staff there opens the archives to me, and each time they do, I leave with scanned records that reveal the real history of easily the most resilient, amazing tribe in our country.

In *The Tree That Bends*, Dr. Patricia Wickman comments that immersing herself in Tribal culture didn't suddenly make her want to wear turquoise. Often, as I've struggled to accept and recant the history of this striking tribe, I've felt the need to assert the same: wanting to decolonize history doesn't mean I want to become Seminole. They've had a horrible battle to get to where they are, and no one would choose their heartbreak and loss. I do, however, feel a compulsion to help set the wrong history right, to shout the real history from the trees or, in this case, from the trees made into the pages of this book. Over that year— and still—I find myself fixating on the Tribe and how they've survived in a hostile, beautiful land, pushed there by a murderous, lying new nation. It's made me question everything I think I know about history, and about our first Americans. As I've sat in their archives and read the few Euro-American historians who have cared enough to learn the Tribe's true history, I've realized that the Tribe's very existence, in the most wonderful, harshest place on the planet—the Everglades—is a tribute to the human will to survive. It's also a credit to a handful of remarkable Seminoles who were willing to risk their lives instead of bending to the will of these unwanted immigrants.

Most Floridians know of Osceola, or Billy Bowlegs. Fewer realize there were three Billy Bowlegs, or why they know the name. And fewer still know of Abiaka, who so infuriated Euro-Americans that they often simply called him "The Devil."

Even fewer people, I would imagine, have heard of Emateloye Estenletkvte. If you Google her name, you'll get not even a full page of results, which reflects a tragic determination to erase powerful women from history. Euro-Americans called her Polly Parker—perhaps her real name was too troublesome. Google "Polly Parker" and "Seminole," and you'll get slightly more than 1,200 results. By comparison, a search for Billy Bowlegs (whose real name was Holata Micco) returns a quarter million hits on Google.

We don't know nearly enough about Emateloye. No one knows exactly when she was born, only that when she died in 1921, she was more than a century old. No census lists her. History doesn't tell us how educated she was. It doesn't tell us what her hopes and dreams were, when or where she was born, who her parents were, or when, precisely, people started calling her Polly Parker.

But names and dates don't always matter. What matters is this: Emateloye may have been born with a price on her head; the US government started actively hunting southeastern Indians at the onset of the second decade of the nineteenth century, and although history books talk of three discrete Seminole Wars, historians at the Seminole Tribe of

Florida will show you history that proves that between 1811 and the start of the Civil War, there was never a time when the US government wasn't trying to capture and kill Florida Indians. They used whatever means necessary, from flying a false flag of peace to lure Osceola to capture, to forcing Creek or Cherokee to help the military hunt for other Seminole.

The Seminole had a history of evading the US military; the stories of their resilience and records of the ways they outsmarted soldiers should be a book of its own. Mothers would hide their babies under palm fronds to keep them from the United States soldiers; Seminole soldiers would hide in the mangroves, a thoroughly unwelcoming tree for an advancing army but a wonderful cloak for those repelling invaders; Abiaka masqueraded through army camps as a simple fisherman, where he would learn of upcoming attacks.

The second phase of the Seminole War proved, dollar for dollar, the costliest war the United States had ever waged. Some accounts suggest the war cost $30 million—more than the country's national budget at the time.[2] Adjusted for 2021 inflation, that's almost $873 million. Nevertheless, the US government was playing a numbers game, and also playing a dirty game—they would capture women and children, which would bring out the men, and then soldiers would take them, too.

In 1858, they captured the young woman known to her clan—Bird Clan—as Emateloye Estenletkvte. Lucy Tiger, Emateloye's only daughter, told historian Albert DeVane in an oral interview that General Harney and his men captured her mother somewhere near Lake Placid, between Lake Istokpoga and Parker Island. From there, soldiers loaded Emateloye, along with thirty other Seminole, in ox carts and brought them to Tampa, then called Fort Brooke. At that point, they brought Emateloye to Egmont Key, a small island in the mouth of Tampa Bay. From 1857 to 1858, this island served as a concentration camp for Florida Indians, a stopover on the Trail of Tears as the United States stole them from their homes and moved them to the Oklahoma Territory.

Encyclopedia Britannica defines a concentration camp as an "internment centre for political prisoners and members of national or minority groups who are confined for reasons of state security, exploitation, or punishment, usually by executive decree or military order. Persons are placed in such camps often on the basis of identification with a particular ethnic or political group rather than as individuals and without benefit either of indictment or fair trial."

The US government captured and imprisoned Emateloye and her kin for reasons they deemed "state security." More plainly stated, for Manifest Destiny, as in "we need all the land, even the swampland, and God wants us to take it." They did so by executive decree; President Andrew Jackson signed the Indian Removal Act into law in 1830. The US government placed Emateloye and other Seminole in the camp at Egmont Key based on their Seminole ethnicity—and no other reason—without benefit of any judicial process.

On the morning of May 5, 1858, the last "voyage of tears" would set sail. We do not know how long Emateloye spent imprisoned on Egmont Key or how many of her tribe she watched perish there. Emateloye's daughter also told DeVane that, on the morning the Seminole imprisoned on Egmont Key saw "the black plume of smoke arising from *Grey Cloud*, the ship that would take them away from home forever, in the distance, they were a sad and depressed band of Indians.

"The thoughts of leaving the home of their childhood, their chickees, log smoke campfires, and the ever-cooking pot of coontie soffka, the morning call of the turkey gobbler, whooping crane, the chase and hunt, the hammock fields of pumpkins and corn, the bark of the fox, the howl of the wolf, the scream of the panther were all sweet music—'The Call of the Wild.' The burial spot of their fathers, mothers, brothers, and sons—their Florida, which they were about to leave."

That early summer day, US soldiers forced Emateloye Estenletkvte and 133 other Seminole aboard the *Grey Cloud*. This was not the first time soldiers had captured Emateloye, but it would be the last. The US first captured a teenaged Emateloye early in the second phase of the Seminole War, along Florida's east coast, but released her. They captured her once again, later in the same phase of the war, along with her eventual husband, Chai, and forced them to help the military scout for other Seminole. Emateloye led the soldiers through the Everglades on a fool's mission, seemingly unable to find other members of their tribe. Nevertheless, she earned her freedom.

When soldiers captured Emateloye for a third time, she knew they would not let her go, or that they would not allow her to earn her freedom. She also knew she would not leave her home. They forced her onto the ship, and though she had no choice but to go, she did have a plan.

Once soldiers loaded them onto the *Grey Cloud,* the families would stay on the ship until it reached the mouth of the Mississippi River at

New Orleans. From there, more soldiers would force them onto a river steamer up the Mississippi River to Arkansas, where they would then march them along the Arkansas River—some 300 miles—on the now-named Trail of Tears, into the Oklahoma Territory. Before the *Grey Cloud* would reach New Orleans, where soldiers would march them away from the Florida home they'd enjoyed for millennia, though, the ship had to stop for wood to fuel the rest of the trip to the Mississippi River. The *Grey Cloud* stopped at St. Mark's, south and slightly west of Florida's present-day Tallahassee capital, near Apalachee Bay.

When the boat stopped, Emateloye told a soldier some of her kin were ill. She could, she said, help heal them—but she didn't have the herbs and plants she needed to do so. If, she said, she could be permitted to get off the boat, with a few assistants, they could gather enough roots and herbs to heal the ill and get them healthy enough to make the trek to their new home in Oklahoma.

The soldiers agreed, and Emateloye and some twelve other Seminole women left the *Grey Cloud*. The US government sent a single guard with them. Once Emateloye and the rest of the Seminole were far enough away from the boat, she gave a signal. We don't know, exactly, what this signal sounded like, whether it was a shrill whistle or a throaty call. It doesn't matter; the women knew it, and on her signal, they scattered. The one guard had no chance of capturing them all. He didn't capture Emateloye, and she and either six or seven women (the history isn't clear) disappeared into the forested swamp.

When night fell, the birds called to one another—but so did the women, mimicking the birds' cries. To a soldier unaccustomed to Florida's wilderness, the call of the night birds might all sound the same, but to Polly and the other Florida women, some of the calls were not like the others. They called to one another and reunited under a sky lit only by a waning gibbous moon. Even then, they did not speak, for fear of recapture, but instead began moving silently south.

That night, Emateloye grew gravely ill. She told the others to leave her, because she couldn't keep their pace and feared she would be the cause of them all getting captured. They refused, and when the sun rose, they hid her in the hardwood swamps while they carefully explored the area to find the best way home.

For the first three nights, the women would help Emateloye as they all progressed first east, then south, but soon, they all grew increasingly weak; for fear of detection, they wouldn't build a fire, choosing instead to eat only wild berries they found in the swamp. On the fourth night, they fashioned a spear and caught a few garfish, a sweet but bony fish. They roasted them over a small fire, their first real meal since escaping the white men. Their pace continued southward; eventually, they made their way to Lake Okeechobee, where they found their old hunting camp, burned and charred. In the ashes, they found a pot; in the sawgrass, they found a canoe, hidden from sight.

That canoe carried them home, the final leg of a 400-mile journey. Emateloye and the women reunited with what remained of their clans.

The US government had gutted the remaining tribe. Harney, known for his brutality in the West, had cut his teeth on killing Seminoles. By some accounts, fewer than 100 Indians remained; an Indian Agent known only as A. M. Wilson wrote in 1887 that 269 Indians remained in the Everglades, although his numbers suggested 200 men, leaving few women to continue the lineage.[3]

Emateloye—today, most people outside the Tribe call her Polly Parker—lived to be more than one hundred years old, and, after her return home, she had a daughter, Lucy. Lucy had a daughter, and that daughter had five children, who collectively had seventeen children.

By 1963, DeVane wrote that the Seminole numbered 1,200 and that an astonishing 20 percent of the now federally recognized Tribe could trace its lineage to Emateloye.

Today, the Seminole Tribe of Florida has more than 4,000 members. It remains the only tribe that never signed a so-called peace treaty with the US government.

The voyage that tried to take Emateloye out of Florida would be the final voyage of the *Grey Cloud* on the Trail of Tears; the United States had a larger issue than the few remaining Indians in South Florida. As the US turned its attention to the Civil War, Emateloye, her clan, and the few others remaining lived a quiet, harsh existence in the Everglades.

The *Tampa Tribune,* in 1956, wrote about Emateloye's daring escape—by then, Euro-Americans called her Polly Parker—labeling it "both thrilling and inspiring—from her standpoint exemplifying supreme loyalty to her people and her native land."[4]

For the future of the Seminole Tribe of Florida, Emateloye's escape was all that—and more.

Only after, as Florida historian Gary Mormino likes to say, the invention of air conditioning and DDT did Florida's population grow, and this time the Florida Indians found themselves fighting a new threat from Euro-Americans: development. Development and agriculture would contaminate their land and cut them off from their historic means of survival: gardening and fishing.

But, because Emateloye and the other women ran from the soldiers, hid in the wilderness, and found their way back home, the Tribe had enough women to raise families, and ninety-nine years after Emateloye and the other women escaped, their descendants would meet under a live oak tree in Hollywood, Florida. Under the shade of that oak, the Tribe created a Tribal government, one the United States would recognize.

The Tribe would fight the United States one last time—this time, in court—to assert that sovereignty. In 1979, they won that fight, which allowed gaming on sovereign land. When they prevailed, they found their path out of poverty—and in so doing, showed that path to every other tribe in the United States. Today, the Hard Rock casinos provide for the Tribe; the proceeds go directly to Tribal members, but they also fund schools on Tribal land, infrastructure, and help provide free, clean drinking water for anyone living on Tribal land.

The life the Seminole enjoyed before Spanish conquistadors brought Europeans to Florida looks little like it did six hundred years ago. They have a fraction of their land, and threats to their way of life still exist, this time environmental as well as racial and governmental.

Nevertheless, Emateloye and the women who escaped with her found a path through Florida, back home, and in doing so, forged a path to the future.

And that, indeed, is the most spectacular thing of all.

ACKNOWLEDGMENTS

It's not uncommon for people to say, "You're so lucky" when they learn I earn my living as a writer. Luck has nothing to do with it: it's a little talent, a lot of work, and a huge team of people who inspire me, make my writing better, and support me through what other authors know to be a love/hate relationship with our vocation.

Brad Bertelli started as a professional acquaintance and has become a dear friend—who always takes the time to read whatever I've written. Brad's written a mostly fictional book about skunk apes, *The Florida Keys Skunk Ape Files,* that gives me joy to read again and again. He also introduced me to David Sloan, without whom I would not have had nearly as interesting an intro to this book. I highly recommend finding a conch shell and drinking bubbly wine from it.

If you've read this far, it's no shock that I'm thanking Carlton Ward, for always saying yes when I ask to interview him, meet me near a swamp, or pick his brain. Mallory Lykes Dimmitt, too, made the chapter on the Florida Wildlife Corridor a better one, as did Laurie McDonald.

Seth Bramson fact-checked my chapter on the Henrys (he's the author of *The Greatest Railroad Story Ever Told: Henry Flagler & the Florida East Coast Railwuy's Key West Extension*) and always has a moment for me to double-check a Henry fact.

The late, great Dave Byers taught eighth-grade me about the Great Depression and the WPA, and I wish he were alive today to know what an impact a truly wonderful teacher can make. (Not so much my tenth-grade language arts teacher, who, when I told her my dreams, laughed at me and told me I'd never be a writer. Fortunately, wonderful teachers like Frank Black, Joanne Roby, and Greg Byrd later undid that damage.)

Later, Dr. Jerry Smith showed undergraduate Cathy the wonders of roaming around the wild parts of Florida, setting me on a path that would ultimately lead me through the Everglades, near juvenile cotton-mouths, and to the Florida Studies program. Never underestimate the impact a truly wonderful teacher can make on a life.

I met Kelli Umstead through a mutual friend who thought we'd enjoy each other's company, and, almost two decades later, we still do. She drove every street in Eatonville with me—it is a true friend who will brave I-4 traffic on a Friday with you—and helped me talk through how I wanted to capture a moment of the town's history.

My friends Joe and Sandy Mitchell, Ken Proctor, Sandy Sigmond, and Tracy Gayton not only did *not* die in the swamp with me, we shared a story I'll tell for the next forty years. As for tour guide Ramsey, well, buddy, I hope you've eased into Florida by now. Thanks for saving the snake from my foot—and getting us out of the swamp (eventually).

Jack Davis and Peggy MacDonald both gave me small details about their respective Marjories, making these giants more real to me—and my readers.

At the Sebring Historical Society, staff pulled out boxes of Albert DeVane's papers, and in those handwritten pages I found the details of Emateloye Estenletkvte's daring escape. At the Smathers Library in Gainesville, Jim Cusick—who also fact-checked my chapter on Florida's forgotten colonies— pulled relevant DeVane papers for me, as well. His book, *The Other War of 1812*, paints a startling history of what actually happened in Florida in the early part of the nineteenth century. It's not light reading, but I highly recommend it.

The Seminole Tribe of Florida offers endless testament to the power of determination, resistance, and persistence. Tina Osceola deserves more than gratitude. Paul Backhouse opened my eyes about everything I thought I knew about Florida's first people. Dave Scheidecker had patience beyond measure in reading eight drafts of the Emateloye Estenletkvte story. If I have something wrong about this heroic woman, it's my fault alone, but Dave agonized over my facts alongside me, and I could not have written this chapter without him.

At one point, I told the press I was trashing this book, and it was Craig Pittman who talked me off the ledge and encouraged me to keep going. Craig wrote three books in the time it took me to write this one—but without his baffled encouragement (his exact words were, "Why don't you just *finish* it?"), I wouldn't have a book at all. If you've never read one of Craig's books, you should. He's a vocal cheerleader for my books, and for Florida writers everywhere. Florida needs more writers like Craig, who believes a rising tide lifts all boats (even if we could use fewer dad jokes sometimes!).

Rick Kilby, yet another fabulous Florida author, co-hosts the *Florida Spectacular* podcast with me, and he's supported me in the best possible way another author can: he has never once asked me when I thought I might finish the book. It's a joy to hop on a podcast with him and Florida-splain every week, and a pleasure to read whatever he's written (I never ask about his next book, either).

Andy Furman made both my books better with his gentle but firm critiques and questions. New Floridians should get a copy of his book *Bitten* at the border.

Gary Mormino gave life to my Florida dreams at USF St. Petersburg. He is a true Florida treasure, and I'm fortunate beyond measure to know him. I may have invented the term "Florida-splaining," but he perfected the action. The highest compliment I've received was when a colleague told me, "You know, you're starting to sound like Gary."

For the second time, my editor, Sian Hunter, guided me through what I'm assuming was, for her, a painful and protracted editing process, and I'm hoping she's forced to do it a third time, because she's a gentle, amazing, gifted soul who makes me look like I know what I'm doing out here.

Calypso helped me write this book, in her own dachshund way—she travels the state with me and snoozes next to me while I write about traveling the state. Her coonhound companion, Banyan, also spent some time on the road with me. Although markedly less relaxed than Calypso, Banyan does romp through Florida's wild bits with joyful abandon.

I said my career is not the result of luck, but that's not wholly true: I lucked out with my parents. Both my mom and my dad told me stories when I was little. My dad told more fanciful ones, about penguins in race cars and the like, while my mom told more moralistic ones, about one sister who was good and one who was naughty, but types of stories, without my parents realizing it, that made me want to tell stories as well as they told those. If this book makes you chuckle or cry, gets you angry or gives you hope, the credit goes wholly to them.

My amazing, devoted, patient husband not only read each chapter and gave me feedback, this brave man did it while I was menopausal and vacillated between tears and rage at the slightest provocation. That's not why I love him beyond measure, but I should publicly thank him for that courageous act of love.

Finally, as with the first book, the panther's share of what makes this book worth reading is a state that is, in a word, spectacular. Stay sexy, Florida.

NOTES

Chapter 1. Florida Springs

1 USGS Fact Sheet FS-151–95, May 1995, https://pubs.usgs.gov/fs/1995/0151/report .pdf.

2 https://pubs.usgs.gov/ha/ha730/ch_g/G-text6.html. Among many, many others.

3 "West Central Florida's Aquifers," Southwest Florida Water Management District, March 2007, https://ufdcimages.uflib.ufl.edu/WC/02/84/15/29/00001/WC02841529 .pdf.

4 http://coastgis.marsci.uga.edu/summit/aquifers_fla.htm.

Chapter 2. Forgotten Colonies

1 *Pensylvania* Gazette (Philadelphia: B. Franklin and H. Meredith; microform), October 7, 1731; S. Urban, "Ship News This Month," *Gentleman's Magazine: Or, Monthly Intelligencer* (London: F. Jefferies, 1731), 265

2 *Pensylvania* Gazette (Philadelphia: B. Franklin and H. Meredith; microform), October 7, 1731.

3 Really, it's worth a read. If you aren't reading this as an ebook, it's worth typing in the address: https://www.ncbi.nlm.nih.gov/pmc/articles/PMC3711623/. Dr. Evan M. Graboyes and Dr. Timothy E. Hullar, "The War of Jenkins' Ear," *Otology and Neurotology* 34, no. 2 (2013): 368–72.

Chapter 7. Hurricanes

1 Eliot Kleinberg, *Black Cloud: The Deadly Hurricane of 1928* (Cocoa: Florida Historical Society Press, 2004), 345.

2 https://www.weather.gov/images/mfl/history/1926_hurricane_WB01.jpg; https://www.weather.gov/images/mfl/events/1926hurricane/1926_hurricane_WB02.jpg.

Chapter 8. Florida Wildlife Corridor

1 https://www4.swfwmd.state.fl.us/springscoast/blackbear.shtml.

2 https://www.businessobserverfl.com/article/florida-regains-its-population-growth -mojo;https://www.bizjournals.com/tampabay/news/2019/07/25/florida-growth-to -top-300–000-peoplc-a-year.html.

Chapter 9. Archbold

1 Fred E. Lohrer, *John A. Roebling, II (1867–1952), Builder of the Red Hill Estate (1929–1941), Lake Placid, Florida. A Brief Biography and the Red Hill Estate* (Venus, FL: Archbold Biological Station, 2005); https://www.archbold-station.org/documents/publicationspdf/JARoebling2-biography.pdf.
2 https://www.archbold-station.org/html/aboutus/r_archbold/archbold.html.
3 https://www.fws.gov/panamacity/resources/EasternIndigoSnakeFactSheet.pdf.
4 https://www.archbold-station.org/html/research/herpetology/herpetol.html.

Chapter 10. The Everglades

1 https://www.southfloridaparks.org/big-cypress-national-preserve/fire-destroys-historic-monroe-station-big-cypress/.
2 https://michaelkleen.com/2017/07/12/abandoned-oasis-ochopees-monroe-station/.
3 https://www.nps.gov/bicy/learn/news/historic-monroe-station-destroyed-by-fire.htm.

Chapter 11. The Nature Conservancy's Disney Wilderness Preserve

1 https://floridadep.gov/sites/default/files/1-CattleVats_19Aug16_1.pdf.
2 Florida Center for Instructional Technology at USF, https://fcit.usf.edu/florida/lessons/de_leon/de_leon1.htm.
3 Florida Public Archaeology Network at the University of West Florida: http://www.flpublicarchaeology.org/anthro/shipwreck/spanish_presence.htm.
4 https://www.floridamemory.com/learn/exhibits/photo_exhibits/ranching/; https://www.fdacs.gov/Agriculture-Industry/Livestock/Cattle-Bovine/Cracker-Cattle-and-Cracker-Horse-Program.
5 Kyle S. VanLandingham, "Pioneer Families of the Kissimmee River Valley," 1976, https://www.lamartin.com/history/pioneer_families_kissimmee_river_valley.htm.
6 Helen Wells, "Origin and Development of Osceola County" (historical narrative), ca. 1939, State Archives of Florida.
7 "The Disney Wilderness Preserve Story," Nature Conservancy, undated,https://njurbanforest.files.wordpress.com/2014/03/dwp-story-for-emailing.pdf.
8 Jim Robinson, "Land Baron Opened the Door for Disney World," *Orlando Sentinel,* July 19, 1998, https://www.orlandosentinel.com/news/os-xpm-1998-07-19-9807190376-story.html.
9 https://www.orlandosentinel.com/business/os-bz-disney-osceola-ranch-purchase-20190109-story.html.
10 Osceola County Property Appraiser, https://ira.property-appraiser.org/Property Search_services/parcelPdf/?pin=292729000000100000.
11 https://www.theledger.com/article/LK/20141129/News/811287249/LL.
12 http://www.cooperativeconservation.org/viewproject.aspx?id=661.
13 https://d23.com/a-to-z/disney-wilderness-preserve-the/.

Chapter 13. Emateloye Estenletkvte

1 https://fcit.usf.edu/Florida/docs/f/florbrit.htm.

2 Michigan State University, http://projects.leadr.msu.edu/youngamerica/exhibits/show/seminolewar/aftermath.

3 Willard Steele, former STOF historian: https://sanborntraiphumanities.files.wordpress.com/2015/10/abriefseminolehistory.pdf.

4 "US Soldiers Led Indian Evangeline into Exile; She Escaped and Made Her Way Back to the Everglades," *Tampa Tribune*, April 1, 1956, 69.

INDEX

Cathy Salustri earned her master's degree in Florida studies from the University of South Florida St. Petersburg, which, to those who know her, is no great surprise, given her intense passion for all things Florida. Her first book, *Backroads of Paradise*, chronicles Cathy's more-than-5,000-mile road trip along Florida's backroads as she sought forgotten and underappreciated Florida. Not content to see Florida from a car, she also boats, sails, kayaks, paddleboards, hikes, and bikes the Sunshine State. Cathy writes and speaks (she calls it Florida-splaining) about Florida for a living from her home in Gulfport, Florida, which she shares with her hound dogs, cats, her husband, Barry, and more than a few brown anoles who valiantly protect her houseplants from danger. Cathy, Barry, and the dogs leave the cats and anoles to their own devices as they explore Florida in their travel trailer. Contact her at cathy@floridaspectacular.com; follow her on Instagram, Threads, LinkedIn, or X as @cathysalustri; or on Facebook as @salustricathy. You can read more of her travels and thoughts about why Florida's better than any other state at floridaspectacular.com, and listen to her weekly podcast celebrating all things Florida, *The Florida Spectacular*.